TATTOOED
BY
GRIEF

A Faith-Based Approach to Helping
Youth Impacted by Loss

CARI ZORNO

BMM
BALDY MOUNTAIN MEDIA

Produced and packaged by Illumify Group
IllumifyMedia.com

Table of Contents

—⟋⟋⟋—

Introduction

Tattooed by Grief

—◊—

It is worse than I thought.

"In this world you will have trouble." John 16:33

—✺—

The statistics are scary. Between 2013, to 2016 there were at least 205 school shootings in America — an average of nearly one a week.[1]

Motor vehicle crashes are the leading cause of death for US teens. In 2013, 2,163 teens in the United States ages sixteen to nineteen were killed in motor vehicle crashes.[2] That translates into six teens ages sixteen to nineteen died every day as a result of motor vehicle crashes.

Suicide is the second leading cause of death for ages ten to twenty-four.[3] More teenagers and young adults die from suicide than from cancer, heart disease, AIDS, birth defects, stroke, pneumonia, influenza, and chronic lung disease, combined. Tim Clinton, president of American Association of Christian Counselors, September 2016 asked a class of seven hundred college students if they knew someone close to them who had taken his or her life — 95 percent raised their hands.[4]

Each of these statistics is startling but we seem to avoid them. Furthermore, we don't stop to consider that in the shadow of these statistics are siblings, friends,

friends of friends, families and others in the community who hear of the death. All are affected.

A death is like a pebble tossed into a pond, the ripples of grief continue outward affecting dozens and sometimes even hundreds of youth. Youth not only experience the death of their peers but also grieve the deaths of parents, siblings, aunts, uncles, and grandparents.

Grief over loss covers more than just the loss of someone through death. Loss due to failures in school, job losses, relationship breakup and divorce of parents just to name a few also can cause youth to grieve.

If you picked up Tattooed by Grief because you know at least one grieving teen and you desire to walk with him or her, then keep reading. If you are a parent, pastor, youth pastor, counselor, teacher, social worker keep reading. If you volunteer in a youth group, a member of a youth institution or organization, school administrator, neighbor or friend of a teen, keep reading. If you picked it up out of curiosity, then keep reading because it is highly likely that before this year is over your life will intersect with grieving youth.

In my small community we experienced the loss of eight youth within five years, my three children plus five more. These friends died in car accidents, from cancer, or by suicide, school violence, and drug overdose. Mind you, I live in a rural area of less than 50,000 in the foothills outside of Denver.

I wrote *Tattooed by Grief* because my heart ached as I watched the youth in my community struggle with grief. I gathered the lessons I had learned while working as a youth pastor with my husband, facilitating GriefShare groups and from walking with my children's friends. I want to share those lessons with others who walk with youth whose hearts have been tattooed by grief.

It doesn't matter if the loss is a death of a parent, sibling, grandparent, aunt, uncle, or a friend; our society as a whole does not prepare any of us well for loss. Long ago, when a loved one neared death, he or she was taken into the family home until the final breath. There was time to seek and give forgiveness, say final good-byes, and extend love. This is rarely done anymore, and many deaths are sudden, not giving us this opportunity.

I feel that death in present-day America has been whitewashed. When grandparents age to the point of needing constant care, they are frequently placed in assisted living, then into nursing homes. We seldom face death as a family and even more rarely experience grief as a family. Less and less we have the older generation teaching the younger generation how to grieve by their example.

Often the deaths that teens must deal with are sudden. They hang out with friends after Chemistry class on Friday only to be faced with an empty stool in lab on Monday. Few school resources exist to help with closure leaving lots of regrets, and few answers. With the lack of experience and maturity in the surviving friends is amplified.

They are unaware of what constitutes healthy grieving and unsure where to find the answers. Where do they turn for help? Most often they turn to a peer or an adult friend. Those adults and peers need to be ready and equipped to handle the complexity of their grief needs.

Our youth are left in a desolate place without mentors

Grieving youth need help navigating around the loneliness and need someone to walk with them into the unwelcome new reality. *New reality*, there is something almost repulsive about the word *new*. New seems to denote better, improved, fresh, or revised in a good way. This *new* is anything but that; it is different, it is changed, it feels unacceptable, it is painful. That's why you are there.

You can walk with grieving youth into the pain and through the change helping them lean into their grief. They need a safe place to talk without judgment. Safe means no pressure to "get over it" and no pressure to cry or not. They need you to walk with them into what has become their reality showing them the importance of grieving in a healthy way, embracing the loss, and walking through the grief. *Tattooed by Grief* will give you to tools to do that.

> *It was not easy to lose someone you were close to, and was not easy to open up. I wish someone would have pushed me harder to talk about it. I felt alone and abandoned, not because I was alone but because I wouldn't let anyone in to help. I wouldn't ask for help, I wouldn't ask for guidance, but I wanted it . . . I needed it. Trying to figure it out on my own didn't help.* — Brian

Tattooed by Grief is a Grief 101. It does not contain all you need to know, but it contains the basics. Here's what you will find in this book:

- In Chapter One and Two you will hear my story and why I have such a passion for grieving youth.
- In Chapter Three you will learn how grief is unique and why that matters.

- Contained in Chapter Four is what can be expected emotionally in grief. With this information you can assure your teen that they are not going crazy.
- With Chapter Five you will learn the physical effects of grief, get a better understanding how grief affects the whole person, and why the adolescent years extend into the mid-twenties.
- Chapter Six is devoted to the ways they can learn from their grief, develop coping skills, and learn tools so when they walk this path again they will be able to grieve in a healthy manner.
- Facing holidays can carry unique challenges. Chapter Seven covers what those challenges can be and how you can help your teen survive those difficult days.
- In Chapter Eight I will cover additional days and other situations which may require focused attention.
- At one time or another we all ask "Why is there suffering"? In Chapter Nine I will cover four of the most common reasons for suffering. It will not answer this question completely but will give you a foundation of understanding to pass on to youth.
- A death often brings up the question regarding what comes next. In Chapter Ten, I uncover a glimpse of the wonders which wait for us and our loved ones in Heaven.

When teens deal with grief their feelings are intense and they need someone to walk with them. You can't be with them 24 hours a day but Jesus can. He is described as a man of sorrows acquainted with grief. They belong to their creator therefore you cannot rescue them from their grief and you cannot "fix" them. But you can walk with them and *Tattooed by Grief* will help you.

The scriptures contained in *Tattooed by Grief* are there for your reference. Take these truths to heart. Share them in conversation not by chapter and verse but imparting the core truth it contains. Often after a death, youth have a spiritual crisis and may not want to hear Bible verses as if they were a pill to eliminate pain. Spouting scripture may turn them away. Truth is truth and it is good for you to know its source.

My hope is that *Tattooed by Grief* gives you a strong foundation upon which you can help youth learn valuable coping skills, what they can expect in their grief, and then the ability to move forward with their lives.

My prayer for you is that God will equip you with strength to comfort the grieving, patience in the ministry of presence, and the courage to speak his words of assurance and encouragement when that is what is needed. May you *"not grow weary of doing good, for in due season we will reap, if we do not give up." Galatians 6:9 (ESV)*

This is where you come in.

Chapter 1

Where It Began

—⚋—

Prepared yet unprepared.

"Everyone who hears these words of mine and does
them will be like a wise man who built his house on
the rock. And the rain fell, and the floods came, and the
winds blew and beat on that house, but it did not fall,
because it had been founded on the rock."
Matthew 7:24-26 (ESV)

—ɯ—

"**N**O, NO, NO" all other words escaped me as I screamed and beat Nathan's chest. My mind swirled with disjointed thoughts. It can't be, it was just moments ago we sat chatting. The words my husband had shouted from the basement "Call 911, gun shot! Cari don't come down!" echoed in my head. It can't be. "NO, NO, NO!"

I had run to the top of the stairs but was brought to an abrupt stop when my husband pleaded with me to not come down. Turning frantically, I collided with Chris' best friend, Nathan, who wrapped his arms around me. He had been invited to spend the night so he could join Chris and his sister Abby for snowboarding the next day. "No, No, No!"

With Scott's words I knew what had happened. Chris had shot himself.

Abby scrambled for the phone and dialed 911. When they started asking questions she shoved at me. Abby was as wordless as I was. "He shot himself!" I screamed, but the questions continued. "He shot himself. Just come!" I screamed again and hung up the phone. I had no more words. I was forced to say what no parent ever wants to say.

My son had taken his own life.

The Christmas tree with opened presents still beneath taunted me. Abby paced the living room like a caged animal until Nathan reached out an arm and drew her into our circle.

My mind began to flash back to when we first arrived in our small mountain community. Abby was ten, Josh age eight, Beth had just turned five and Chris was coming up on three when we moved up from the city to Bailey. Chris met Nathan shortly after. Nathan spent so much time at our home, he was practically another son.

> *We wanted to live somewhere close enough for Scott to have his city job while we could live a mountain lifestyle. It was a perfect fit. We picked a rural area away from the city smog because of health concerns. Our two middle children, Josh and Beth, were born with a terminal genetic disease, cystic fibrosis. CF affects the lungs and digestive system. We felt we could help the lung issue by giving them cleaner air to breathe and space to run.*

My heart pounded as the sirens stopped at our house. I pushed away from Nathan. My hands were sweating and my thoughts swam. *I'm an EMT I'm supposed to be the one called in to help. What are they saying? No I don't want to know.* Pacing like a trapped lion I now had to stay back and let them work. Confused and panic stricken I glanced down the stairs just as they wheeled Chris out the door. *Oh God no! Lord help us!* They left giving Scott instructions regarding which hospital the Flight for Life chopper was headed. We, including Nathan, piled into our pastor's car and began the one-hour drive to the hospital in silence. There were no words.

My head spun as we were ushered into the Family Waiting Room. Minutes were hours as we sat, prayed, and paced. Friends on the ambulance agency who had heard the call found me at the hospital and circled me with their love and concern. Most of them knew all my kids. They had watched them grow up. Abby and I had joined the agency together seven years before. She and I both became certified as EMTs. She went on to become a CNA. For a short time Josh had been a junior member of the ambulance service. Beth brought smiles and cookies to rescue base whenever she stopped by, and Chris just hung out with the medics anytime he could.

Sitting between Abby and Scott on the couch in the Family Waiting Room, the hole in my heart felt bottomless as I longed for my family to be whole again.

We had homeschooled all the kids which meant we spent the majority of each day together. The kids were either each other's best friends or worst enemies - depending on the moment. The days were spent in books, field trips and working as volunteers somewhere in the community.

At the age of ten, Josh confronted one of his CF doctors with a tough question: "Am I going to die of CF?" That question had been tumbling in his head; he had watched the health of a friend with CF deteriorate, and he needed to know.

The doctor was truthfully blunt: "Yes, everyone with CF dies of CF." He was correct for that time in history, but he didn't realize he had thrown down the gauntlet for my son.

As we exited the clinic, Josh declared under his breath but so I could hear, "Nope, not me. I'm going to find something else to kill me." The challenge had been accepted. My heart grew heavy with what that meant. Josh began living life to its fullest and to the outermost edge.

Josh did dangerous things a young man would want to do. With a cowboy mind set he tried bull riding and bullfighting but quickly lost interest. He joined a local search and rescue team, which incorporated his dad into his adventures. They did all night searches and high angle repelling rescues. Becoming a lifeguard and then an EMT were stepping stones for him to become a volunteer firefighter and then he reached his final goal: joining the Army National Guard as an armorer for Special Forces Airborne.

Chris stood by and watched all Josh's adventures and step by step Josh became a hero to his little brother, Chris.

Oh Josh, I miss you. I miss your smile and you gave such great hugs. I could use one of those right now.

My thoughts were interrupted when the Flight for Life crew stepped into the doorway. After apologizing for interrupting they wanted to assure us that everything possible was being done for Chris. I looked up and realized that the flight nurse was a friend. My heart ached; so many friends had been forced to be a part of my nightmare. She hugged me tight as my pain mixed with hers. When they left I sunk into a chair my face hot with tears.

Scott covered my hands with his but I just couldn't look up as tears wet my lap.

Lord, please spare my son, my youngest one. He is your special gift to us. After Beth was born we weren't going to have any more kids but you blessed us with Chris. Oh Lord, help! You know what is best. Your will, Lord; your will.

Looking for distraction my ears caught the laughter of a little girl in a distant hallway.

Oh Beth, I miss you. I miss your laughter and your sweet spirit. Beth; tall, beautiful, blonde haired, blue eyed and always included in the in crowd but she was driven only by love. She joined the swim team and because of her love to include everyone she was named social butterfly. Her coach commented that with Beth on the team they really had a team. Her heart was for the downtrodden, the underdog, and those who didn't know Christ. The world was her mission field. As a social butterfly she included everyone, which meant our home was always full of love, laughter, and friends.

Though these side trails seemed a good distraction they reminded me that I had been here before. I had already buried two of my four children. I can't bear to bury another! No, Lord. Not again. No, No, No, please help us Lord!

Chapter 2

Not Again

—⁂—

More than I can bear.

"We were crushed and overwhelmed
beyond our ability to endure…
But as a result, we stopped relying on ourselves
and learned to rely only on God."
2 Corinthians 1:8,9 (NLT)

—m—

Only three years had passed since our memorable Thanksgiving conversation. After dinner Beth said "I don't want to die suffocating in a hospital." Beth had recently spent 21 days in the hospital spending a lot of time with her friend April whose health was deteriorating due to CF. The memories of her friend suffering from CF were fresh in her mind.

"If you could tell God how you wanted to die, what would you say?" I asked.

"I want to die fast, so I don't know what takes me from this life to heaven." She answered without hesitation.

Josh agreed with her unreserved answer but added, "I want to die doing something fun, and I don't want to die alone."

Four months later, God granted their requests with brutal mercy. It was brutal on us but merciful on them as the motorcycle they rode slid into oncoming traffic and they both died instantly. In the time it took for the deputy to tell me, "They're both gone," grief etched its painful tattoo on my heart. In that same moment Chris lost his hero and Abby, the big sister protector, became the oldest of two not four. She knew she needed to learn to connect with Chris, eight years younger than her, but first she needed to deal with her grief.

Abby buried her grief in busyness accepting a position as receptionist at a spa in Keystone Ski Resort. She worked days, snowboarded in the evening and joined her work associates in the party scene at night. Slowly she began to slip into depression. A friend helped her to see this and she sought out a counselor for help. Her habits changed and so did her journey as she enrolled in school at Center for Creative Media pursuing a career in media production. This long-buried desire bubbled to the surface. Two years passed since Josh and Beth had died. She was ready to move forward.

Chris made his own way after Josh's death but still following in his brother's footsteps as he joined Search and Rescue and became a Sherriff reserve officer. He climbed mountains in the dark of night then directed traffic when the highway through our town was shut down from a car accident. Even at the young age of seventeen his servant heart connected him with many who served our community.

Shortly after Chris became a deputy reserve our community suffered at the hand of a man who took a classroom in our local high school hostage. While I waited at a rescue staging area across from the high school with an ambulance, Chris helped direct traffic then ran keys from the Sherriff's office to SWAT at the school.

When his help was no longer needed at the Sherriff's office he ran home, changed clothes into his orange Search and Rescue shirt, then took bottles of water to the elementary school. As high school and *middle school students were brought there to safety Chris met them as they unloaded from the buses. Chris became aware of a dad's voice from the crowd behind him.*

"Can anyone help me? I need to talk to a Deputy." His voice was strained.

Chris turned and looked at the dad, "I might be able to help," Chris said, "What do you need?"

"My daughter isn't here," the dad's voice betrayed his fear, "She is still in the school."

"Why do you say that?" Chris asked.

"Because I just got a text from her," he handed Chris his phone, "See, it says 'I love u guys.'" I need to tell a Deputy," His voice now frantic.

"I can get someone for you to talk to at the Sherriff's office." Chris said trying to calm the dad, "Follow me." Chris sprinted to his car for his hand-held radio, and soon he became the connection between the anxious parent of a student still being held and the Sherriff.

Chris was in his element, helping people, unfortunately a student his age died. As with any emotionally traumatic situation; he was impacted. Grief over the deaths of his brother and sister, less than three years prior, was brought back to the surface like a scab being torn from a wound. He struggled silently.

At Christmas, I asked, "Do you want to talk to someone?"

"No, I don't want to bother anyone over the holidays," He replied, "I'll call someone in a couple weeks."

I accepted his answer.

Two days after Christmas Chris spent the day preparing for a fun day on the mountain with Nathan and Abby. Chris loved the process of getting ready. It would take him ten days to prepare for 3-day back-pack trip.

Today was no different. I had spent the day running errands with Abby and he called me seven times to make sure he wasn't forgetting anything. Every call ended in "Thanks mom, I love you." I made sure I answered my phone every time, now I wish I had let it roll onto my voicemail so I would have his voice.

After dinner I had watched as he and Nathan checked over what he had put into the backpack: Snacks? Check. Water? Check. Gloves and helmet liners? Check.

"What about your wrist brace?" I'd interjected.

"Mom, it is so hard to board with that on," Chris retorted.

The conversation became heated but was resolved with a bit of common sense. Chris had broken his wrist last season his first day on the mountain. This was protection from another break.

Somehow the conversation led from his wrist injury to his shoulder aching; then the discussion spiraled as he brought up his heartache. We all felt that deep ache reverberating through this holiday season, the pain of grief over Josh and Beth's death.

"No one understands my pain, I guess I'll," Chris said then paused as he collected his thoughts.

Abby, Nathan and I just sat there waiting for him to finish his sentence.

Suddenly he stood and ran downstairs. I saw Nathan's eyes follow Chris to the stairs as if he had considered following him but he sat back down. Scott had just gone downstairs. I heard the squeak of the wood stove. Scott was putting on another log. Chris' bedroom door slammed, and it was quiet. Below me something hit the wall. "I wish he wouldn't throw things when he was angry." Ran through my mind.

Lord, it had only been 33 months since Josh and Beth had died in that motorcycle accident together. Josh was only 20, engaged and his life ahead of him. Beth was 17, barely hitting her stride with so much to give.

*N*o Lord, not Chris! He's only 17.
I crumbled back into unstoppable tears just as the ER doctor stepped into the room.

"We've done everything we could," he drew in a deep breath, " I'm so sorry for your loss," the doctor said with halting speech.

Awkwardly, he stood there seeming to want to say something more but there were no more words.

"You can stay as long as you want. Again, I am sorry."

I don't remember leaving the hospital or the drive to a friend's house to spend the remainder of the night. Nathan tagged along with us otherwise he would be alone at his house.

Morning slowly made its appearance. Before I even opened my eyes I could tell the snow was still falling through the muted morning light. For a couple seconds all was right with the world, my mind felt peace. Suddenly fire raced through me, searing my heart with unbearable pain.

Bolting to my feet I screamed, "NO! Not Chris! NO, NO"

Scott bound across the bed and threw his arms around me pulling me close to his chest. I crumbled into a sobbing mess. The nightmare of the night was my reality.

After a few nights with our friends Nathan returned home and we received an invitation from a neighbor to stay in their home until we were ready to go home. Scott went back to work after two weeks. I spent my days sitting in the living room of our home. Once Scott got home we'd eat something then back to the neighbors to sleep. Sleeping in our home was far too painful.

One overcast morning, a few weeks after Chris' death, I woke not wanting to get up and seeing no need to even pull the covers off my head. *Now I know how people end up in a mental hospital in the fetal position just humming and rocking.* Truthfully it sounded pretty good.

So what are you going to do? Will you give in or get up and do something with this? I knew it was God speaking to my heart.

I had a decision to make, give in or get up. I knew from my past experience with grief I needed to get up. I thought Chris' suicide had ruined whatever ministry God wanted me to do after Josh and Beth's deaths.

I reached out for God but my prayers seemed to bounce off the ceiling. Day after day I sought to feel him again. My spiritual life was dry and empty. So much had changed.

After Josh and Beth died my connection to God was solid, though the daffodils and hyacinths poking their heads through the dark soil were colorless. The sun rose and set in shades of grey and when it felt darkest my thoughts turned to Him. With eyes closed I'd reach out my arms and He would lift me onto his lap then hold me so close I could rest my cheek on his chest and inhale the fragrance of God.

I knew God was faithful. My daily walks with him were comforting. Jesus walked with me; He grieved with me and laughed with me. When I needed to move forward Jesus would carry me for He had walked through the shadow of death and knew the way. As my emotional strength grew Jesus would hold my hand as I walked through my grief looking at pictures, remembering, and crying. Jesus was closer to me than my next breath.

This time was different.

Oh Lord I need you now. I can't walk this journey without you. I want to feel you.

"Where are you God?" I plead but heard only silence.

"Lord, to make it through this I need you." Followed by more silence. "Where are you?"

My heart pounded, I feared being abandoned, but in my head I knew he would never leave me (Hebrews 13:5). My experience with God after Josh and Beth's deaths was palpable. Now I hung onto that knowledge. Just because the white noise swirling in my head overpowered God's still small voice (1 Kings 19:12) did not mean God wasn't there.

I swung my feet to the floor with resolve

"Ok, I'm getting up."

He carried me through the valley of the shadow of death when I didn't have the strength to put one foot in front of the other after Josh and Beth's deaths. I had faith He would do it again. Psalm 40:1–2 became my life verse:

> *I waited patiently for the Lord;*
> *He inclined to me and heard my cry.*
> *He drew me up from the pit of destruction,*
> *out of the miry bog,*
> *and set my feet upon a rock,*
> *making my steps secure. (ESV)*

He heard my cry and pulled me from the pit and made my steps secure.

Two years passed before the sun began to rise and break up the fog which covered the deep darkness of grief following Chris's death. When I looked around I realized over the last five years our youth community had lost eight peers which included my three children. This left our youth population in shock and they were without mentors to help them cope.

This began my search for a curriculum or book on teen grief to help me form a support group. I poured over book catalogs, curriculum catalogs, and bookstores to only come up empty-handed.

I asked God "Where I do look next?" My heart ached for the teens caught in the shock wave of grief.

I was compelled to write *Tattooed by Grief* in order to help the youth around me. *Tattooed by Grief* is a compilation of where I walked on my grief journey, my experiences as a youth group leader, crisis responder for Samaritan's Purse, Chaplain for the Billy Graham Rapid Response Team, GriefShare facilitator with my husband as well as what I learned both from books and while becoming a Board Certified Master Christian Life Coach with an emphasis on grief, stress, health and wellness.

I pray that *Tattooed by Grief* becomes a resource for you as you mentor and walk with the youth in your community.

Chapter 3

The Uniqueness of Grief

—m—

No one understands!

"Trust in the Lord with all your heart
and lean not on your own understanding."
Proverbs 3:5

Those who have spent any time with teens have heard the words "No one understands!" Many of us have even said it ourselves. This statement is never more true than with grief because grief is unique to each person for each loss.

> *Friends my age didn't know what to say. Some related the experience to losing a family pet, which made me mad. Other people would tell me I needed to move on because it happened a long time ago. Of course, my family and people who knew my brother John, like his girlfriend, would pray for me. —Ashley*

The first step in walking with grieving youth is developing a relationship if one is not already in place. If you are a youth leader, friend, or parent, there is no time like the present to get to know the teens within your circle. You can be the one that makes a difference, not by your abilities but by your availability. Don't wait until someone has experienced a loss to begin. Here are some ideas as you develop relationships with the teens in your life:

- ASK about favorite colors, snack foods, movies, and music genres. Maybe they have a favorite sport or pastime such as playing video games, walking the mall, hiking, or biking. Ask them thought-provoking questions, for example: "If you could sit on a beach or mountain top with someone, who would it be? What would you talk about?
- LISTEN: Learn how to actively listen to them and absorb information rather than thinking about what you will say next. Asking the question "Are you okay?" carries great power and opens communication when you are willing to listen to the answer, even when the answer is tear-filled silence. Give them your full attention. Just a glance at your phone will bring the conversation quickly to a close. Put it away — not just put it down but put it away, at least on silent but preferably off.
- ACT: Take time to do with them the things you learned they enjoy doing. Most teens talk better while doing something. Maybe it is just to sit over a cup of coffee or shoot hoops. Time builds relationships.
- BE PRESENT: Grieving teens need to know there is someone who cares about them. Someone who will listen when they need to talk. Someone who will sit with them when they need to be silent. Someone who will encourage them to play video games, shoot hoops, or just walk the mall when they need to be "normal." They need

someone who doesn't claim to understand but just "gets it."

Getting to know them — really know them — is an art, a lost art. Practice it. You can be the one person willing to come alongside them, someone who will listen to their pain and not try to "fix" it. You can be their behind-the-scenes hero.

These are first steps in knowing what to do for them on those tough days, which we will discuss later. No one cares how much we know until they know how much we care. Relationship is first about sharing the mundane before it graduates to sharing deep inner thoughts and feelings. Give the relationship time, day after day, week after week. Grief is a very long process; there will be lots of opportunities for sharing if you take the time to establish a relationship.

As I walked through our church prior to a service, the tattoos on two young adults caught my eye. I stepped out of my comfort zone and asked, "Would you mind telling me about your tattoos?"

The initial look on their faces was that of shock, but it quickly faded into excitement to tell their stories. "Thanks for asking," one of them said. "We've found that very few people older than us understand tattoos." This began a wonderful conversation. Each tattoo was unique, each of these young adults told me their unique story and shared a different reason for getting their tattoo.

Tattoos have become part of the norm of our society. Over 36 percent of women and 47 percent of men in the United States between the ages of eighteen and thirty-six have at least one tattoo.[5] Some wrap around the upper arm, others are a complete sleeve, or you might only see a corner of another peeking above a collar or behind the ear. Each one is unique in the story behind it.

Grief is as unique as a tattoo, a fingerprint, or a snowflake. Unfortunately, no one will ever fully understand someone's grief—not friends, not parents, not counselors, and not even those who have also experienced the death of that same loved one. God created each of us as unique individuals, with unique relationships. The death of a grandparent, an immediate family member, a close friend, or a pet will each be grieved at a different level.

In *Tattooed by Grief,* we focus on the death of a person, but that of course is not the only type of grief. Teens can experience grief over the death of a dream: not being accepted at a college of choice, a broken engagement, parents' divorce, and the loss of health can all cause grief. If your teen is grieving over one of these, his or her grief can be as intense as if it were a person who died. Please be encouraged to use all of the information in this book to walk with your teen no matter the cause of their grief.

When a family member dies, each member of that family will experience grief unique to him or her as a person and to the relationship he or she had with the deceased. No one else understands because every personality is unique, everyone is in a different place in life, and each relationship with the deceased was unique; making everyone's grief unique.

Those who have also experienced loss may not understand fully, but most will "get it." They get that the sadness is deep and dark. They get that it casts a dense cloud over life. They also get that grief needs a relief valve with times of activity, fresh air, and laughter. They get that it will last longer than anyone wants, and it can wait in hiding and ambush the teen when he or she least expects it.

Teens may find "good-byes" need to be said all over again in special places and events. Just because the grieving teen laughs does not mean he or she is "over it" or "ready to move on."

No one fully understands, but the grieving need to know there are others around who "get it."

The day my two children died, a couple came to our home to extend condolences. As soon as they entered, the husband said, "There are no words," and wrapped his arms around me and held me tight. *"He gets it. Thank you, Lord,"* was the only thought running through my mind. Those four words, "There are no words," brought great comfort.

When youth experience the death of a close friend, this death may be felt as deeply and sometimes even more deeply than the death of a family member. Youth often spend more time with their peers. They interact during the eight hours of school and five days a week, then choose to hang out after school and on weekends. Those relationships become extremely close. Families are the people they see between hanging out with friends and doing homework before heading to bed.

The depth of a teen's grief is not only determined by the family or social connection they had to the one who died. The heart and spirit connection plays a bigger part than you may know.

Two years after Chris died I received a call from Chelsea. She was in Chris' chemistry class and wanted to meet with me. She explained she was a friend of Chris and needed to talk to me. After a lengthy introduction Chelsea attempted to explain her connection to Chris but words fell short.

She felt guilty for grieving so deeply for someone she only attended class with. She felt she needed my permission to grieve. She had tried to convince herself that his death shouldn't matter because they weren't close. Still Chris' death deeply pierced her heart. We spoke for quite a while. I affirmed her grief and we now walk the path of grief together meeting for breakfast regularly.

Personality types respond differently under the stress of grief. Extroverts under stress tend to pull inward and become uncharacteristically quiet. A person who is sullen and detached might simply be an extrovert under stress. Introverts under stress tend to lash out or freak out. A person who is animated and speaking out may in fact be an introvert experiencing stress.[6]

Everyone will walk through sorrow in different ways, at varying speeds, and with diverse depths of feeling. The important focus is to go *through* it, not around it by avoiding or numbing the feelings through self-medication by drugs or alcohol. When grief is buried, avoided, or numbed, it smolders and surfaces later.

> *I tried to keep things held inside, but when I did break down, it was so much worse than when I was open about my loss. One thing I did to express my pain was to journal . . . and some of those words became songs. Music has been therapeutic for me.*
> — Katie

Feelings need to get expressed somehow. Expression of those feelings may take the form of written, drawn, sung, or spoken words. For some, the feelings need to be put into action and can be expressed with dance, painting, or hiking, just to name a few.

Get to know what your teen uses for expression. Grief that is not expressed cannot heal. Bottled up or buried grief may manifest itself in depression, anger, or bitterness, which is harmful to the hurting teen and to those around them. Teens need to be encouraged to be bold enough to share their feelings in a way most comfortable for them.

Grieving is hard work that can only be done in short bursts. It is unhealthy to expect grieving teens to be sad all the time. Help your teen to break the pain into manageable pieces. Teens need healthy releases for the tension and stress of grief.

- Get active: going for a walk, bowling, playing basketball, bike riding, or swimming.
- Give the brain a rest by watching a favorite movie.
- Go to a sporting event.
- Go shopping.
- Play paint ball or miniature golf.

Healthy grief emotions will be a roller coaster ride with peaks and valleys. Be patient. They need to know they are not walking this journey alone. Going through it with support, with community, makes it easier, and knowing there is a group of peers who also "get it" helps them realize they are not alone. If your youth is over 15 years old consider locating a GriefShare group for support. These can be found at www.GriefShare.org.

Grief doesn't make sense. Sometimes a grieving teen may feel disconnected, like a third party watching from a distance. It is common for the mind to feel like it is in hyper drive, like a pinball machine, unable to connect thoughts. Busying themselves with activity or hiding in music and video games may be their fallback mode of coping.

The tattoo of grief on the heart is permanent, but the intense feelings are temporary, though no one ever knows how long they will last since each loss is unique. Teens need to be assured that what they are feeling right now is temporary. Though time drags by at a snail's pace, it is temporary. These feelings will not last forever. Honestly, depending on the relationship with the one who died, it could be either a few months or a few years before they move forward. Once again, everyone's grief is unique.

The human brain doesn't stop developing at the end of adolescence but continues well into the twenties.[7] This contributes to a teen's inability to grasp cause and effect and to understand that what they are feeling is temporary. As you walk with grieving teens, you need to repeat frequently the concept of the temporariness of intense grief feelings to help them grasp they will not feel this way forever.

How will they know they are healing? Grief is an emotional roller coaster. One minute, grieving teens feel really sad, possibly even crying for no reason they can pin down. The next minute a friend tells a joke and they laugh. Sadness and laughter may pass as quickly as they come. This roller coaster ride can continue for quite a while, but eventually the ups stay longer and the downs become shorter.

They will know there is healing when they look back at where they have been and compare it to where they are now. Hearing input from your observation of their grief process or suggesting they read what they wrote in a journal early on may be helpful in giving them a fresh perspective.

The more I opened up about the loss, the lighter the
weight became. As I look back, the sadness, obviously,

did not go away or fade; it just became more endurable. It became something I could live with instead of preventing me from living. — Chelsea

They will know there is healing when they can look back at things they had drawn or written, text messages they had sent, or conversations they had in the beginning and realize that their moods are improving. For this reason it is important for youth to document how they feel physically, spiritually, and emotionally at the end of each week. Documenting today will help them tomorrow. It is recorded in black and white that they are healing. I encourage the use of a grief journal in which to write what they feel and how they are processing life. Watch for small improvements you can point out to them. Tracking improvement can be very encouraging. Yes, hormones also play a part in the roller coaster, but improvements will be seen.

If the sadness is deep for a long time, meaning several months, please encourage them to speak to a trained counselor. Listen for a feeling that life is hopeless or totally meaningless, they may be sliding into depression. Depression locks teens into believing their emotional pain is a permanent state with no way out. They need help escaping this trap. Chronic depression can lead to suicidal thoughts, which they may attempt to conceal. Sharing their intentions with one friend should be taken seriously and needs to be addressed immediately. Trained counselors can help them refocus and lift this darkness.

I was emotionless and blank. I would just go back to my barracks room and sit in the dark and just listen to music or play video games 'cause I could let out some of the suppressed emotions. It took a long time to talk to anybody about it. The only person I can remember talking to was my fiancé. Having someone to talk to about it helped. – Brian

Another key to understanding the unique grief of youth is knowing about the many physical changes they are going through just being teens. Their bodies change radically. For some their wardrobes can't keep up. When their bodies ache from the physical changes and the heart aches from loss, life can be overwhelming. For others, their emotions will take them on roller coaster rides even apart from grief. They may already feel they are going crazy. They need friends and adults who are willing to come alongside them, spend time with them, listen to them, and then listen some more. What they are feeling is common. It is important for them to know they are normal. Just like growing pains, the grief will subside. They will heal.

Remember, each person's grief is unique. You will see both ends of the spectrum regarding many of the areas I mention. Your job is to be aware of your teen's "normal" before the death and how it has changed. Did they used to be introverts and now they are lashing out at friends? Maybe they were extroverts and now just want to sit in the corner. They don't feel like themselves and don't act as they normally would. This can cause them great concern.

You can be the one on the outside looking in to help them see that because of grief, all they are experiencing is common. This is important for teens to hear because they want to know they're not weird or going crazy.

With the teens I walk alongside, we make journals. I encourage them to use an inexpensive composition book and cover it with a collage of their own drawings or pictures, phrases, and words cut from magazines that remind them of their loved one. This journal becomes the place to write their thoughts, poems, stories, and pictures of what they were feeling at a given time during their grief journey. They then can go back to these journals and see their progress over time. The outside of the journal represents not only how unique their loved ones were but also their own uniqueness.

The following are some situations that bring new forms of uniqueness to the grieving process.

Sibling Grief

Sibling death has its own set of struggles in addition to what is commonly anticipated in grief. Sibling death has been classified as disenfranchised loss, meaning that society fails to classify the surviving sibling's grief as a legitimate loss.[8] When a sibling dies, a child or teen's grief is sidelined while everyone is concerned about how the parents are dealing with the death of a child. Teens need to be asked the question "How are you doing?" or "Are you Okay?" before they are asked, "How are your parents?"

Often the surviving children experience a loss of identity. My daughter experienced a huge change going from being the oldest of four children to being an only child over a three-year period. She had to learn her new place in the family.

When a sibling dies, part of one's story is gone. The surviving sibling has lost a special connection with the past. During family conversations, "Do you remember when_____?" loses its punch when the sibling with whom he or she had this experience with is no longer there to tell his or her side of the story. At family events and gatherings important parts of stories are difficult to tell. Encourage your grieving teen to tell the story anyway, as he or she remembers it. Telling stories which include the deceased sibling helps the teen to accept his or her new reality. These stories also keep the memories of the loved one alive.

Losing a sibling can also mean feeling like they lost a part of themselves.[9] Several realities come into play:

- Possibly the one person to whom the teen told all his or her secrets is gone.
- The weight of home responsibilities changes and grows.
- Sibling-hood is supposed to be forever.

Loss of a sibling represents more than one loss. Siblings are supposed to be bridesmaids or groomsmen, hunting or fishing partners. The death of a sibling leaves a huge hole in a teen's life that will never be filled. Whenever a milestone is reached grief rears its head again. A brother or sister that would have been there to celebrate with the teen is no longer there.

The surviving siblings want to grieve, they may even know they should grieve, but Mom and Dad are falling apart and possibly neither is able to parent. Sometimes teens are wrongly told, "Be strong for your parents." This can cause them to shelve their grief in order to hold things together, to be "the parent," until their parents get a handle on life again.

Putting grief on hold is like putting a pot of soup to simmer on the back burner and ignoring it; eventually the soup cooks down and burns to the bottom of the pan making it difficult to clean up. When grief is put on hold, it can surface later in other areas of their lives such as depression, anger, drug or alcohol abuse, or isolation. This makes grief difficult to "clean up." Here are some helpful guidelines to remember:

Resist the temptation to ask how the parents are doing; everyone else has that covered. Youth need to know you care about how *they* are doing.

- Ask for stories and memories involving their sibling.
- Encourage them to express their grief when they are with you.

The death of a best friend can present like the death of a sibling. Chris and Nathan had known each other since they were three. They did everything together, including evading big brothers who wanted to use them for water balloon target practice. When Chris died, a part of Nathan died too. He lost not only his best friend but his backpacking partner, fishing buddy, and the one who was going to enlist in the army with him. To Nathan, Chris was a brother, but his loss was a disenfranchised loss, not recognized by his family or society. To them Chris was "just" a friend.

As the one walking alongside, you need to be aware of the intensity of your teen's grief over the loss of a close friend. Help your teen to share about his or her relationship with the one who died.

Parental Cautions

Parents grieving the death of a child struggle to meet their surviving teen's needs. Once the parents are beyond the initial shock, there are pitfalls they need to consider. Steps should be taken to avoid these for the emotional health of the family. These pitfalls were shared with me by a teen grief support group.

- Idolizing the dead child while ignoring the living one. This causes the living to question their value and their parents' love.
- Praising the dead child and drawing negative comparisons (Why can't you be more like _____?). When the deceased child is seen as the perfect child, the surviving children can't live up to those expectations.
- Smothering or overprotecting the living child. A bird held too tightly wants all the more to fly.
- Burying the memories of the dead child along with the burial of the body (packing everything away to avoid the pain). To heal well, grief needs to be walked through, not avoided.

You may be able to open a window of insight for the parents. Parents need to be made aware of these pitfalls and the negative effects they have on the living children.

The Cause of Death affects the Grief Process

Long-term illness — Grief over loss often will begin at the diagnosis and continue after death. Family may endure pain-filled years of watching their loved one wither away. Grief after the death may be shorter, and it may not. Either way, it is not any less painful. Despite thinking there was plenty of time to prepare, there may still be shock and disbelief.

Sudden death — With a traumatic death, grief hits like a ton of bricks. Survivors are unprepared. Emotional trauma, disbelief, shock, and numbness can be experienced even more deeply. Some may describe this as watching the world detached, like they are watching themselves go through life on television. Reality feels surreal. When a death is traumatic, an *emotional* traumatic brain injury may be experienced. This is covered later in the chapter about the physical aspects of grief.

Compound Grief

Grief can be magnified by extenuating factors:

- When someone takes his or her own life, it doubles grief. Teens will grieve for the death of their loved ones and grieve for the pain that led them there.
- When there are multiple losses, it is difficult for the brain to differentiate and separate grief. Each death needs to be grieved, but the memories are stacked, so it takes longer to move forward.
- When a loved one is murdered, the death is revisited as court dates are set, postponed, rescheduled, and postponed again.
- If there was a fight just before the death, regret and guilt complicate grief.

Compound grief often needs professional counseling to help the teen process his or her loss.

> *"Be merciful to me, Lord, for I am in distress;*
> *my eyes grow weak with sorrow,*
> *my soul and my body with grief.*
> *My life is consumed by anguish and my years by groaning;*
> *my strength fails because of my affliction,*
> *and my bones grow weak."*
> *— Psalm 31:9–10*

Grief affects every part of the body. King David in this Psalm spoke of every part of his being; his eyes, his soul, his body, his bones, and even his life were consumed by his grief. David cried out to God about what he was experiencing, yet he always came back to trust in God as the answer: "But, I trust in you, Lord; I say, 'You are my God'" (Psalm 31:14).

Chapter 3 key points:

- Take time to connect with your teen. Ask— Listen— Act— Be Present.
- Grief is unique; everyone experiences it in his or her own way.
- Remind grieving teens they are not alone.
- The intense feelings of grief are temporary.
- Grief is a process, not an event; it takes time to heal.

Chapter 4

The Emotions of Grief

—ɯ—

My life is ruined forever!

"I am worn out from my groaning.
All night long I flood my bed with weeping
and drench my couch with tears."
Psalm 6:6

—ɯ—

A tattoo leaves a permanent mark on the skin, grief leaves a permanent mark but its mark is on the heart. Pain will soften as a grieving teen heals, but it will never go completely away. Their memories will change from painful to grateful, but they will not forget their loved ones. The intense feelings of grief are temporary, but the loss is permanent.

The death of a close loved one is similar to an amputation. For an amputee, a part of that person is gone, never to return. At first the pain experienced at the loss of a limb is stabbing and sometimes incapacitating. The healing is slow, but eventually the limb is fitted with a prosthetic. At first the prosthetic rubs and chaffs, but it conforms and becomes usable, though bumping the wound can still cause pain. Slowly the amputee is able to adjust to his or her "new normal" to move forward in life. One thing is for sure: the amputee never forgets he or she once had two hands and two feet.

After the death of a loved one, the teen, like the amputee, realizes a part of him is gone forever. At first the pain is stabbing and often overwhelming. Slowly healing takes place, but "bumping" the wound of grief can still bring pain. "Bumping" can be hearing the loved one's favorite song or anticipating an upcoming birthday or holiday. Over time and with work, the grieving teen adapts to the way life is now. Eventually he learns coping skills and is able to move forward yet never once forgetting the sibling, parent, or best friend. The intense pain will not last forever.

The word "forever" has a different meaning to adults than it has for teens. Adults usually look back over their past experiences and then project into the future if the emotions they have now or the situation they are currently dealing with will continue. Adults recognize that very few things continue forever, especially emotions.

The teen brain is still growing and is not fully formed until the mid 20s. Because their brains are not fully formed, teens have a difficult time seeing the finiteness of feelings. What they feel right now is what they believe they will feel absolutely forever. You can bring them perspective.

They may have been on top of the world; life had never been better. Then they receive an email from a boyfriend or girlfriend announcing a breakup. Devastation is now the feeling that will last "forever," according to them. They have already forgotten the happiness of earlier that day. It is good to remind them of past disappointments and losses they got through. This is a time for developing coping skills, teaching them they will get through this too.

My son Chris had declared to his best friend the day he died, "Life has never been better, Christmas wasn't as hard as I expected, and I got everything I wanted." Two hours later he took his own life overshadowed with the pain of remembering his brother who had died nearly three years prior. Chris, overwhelmed with a temporary feeling, chose a permanent solution.

Teens already deal with hormonal influx affecting the emotions. With a still developing brain, the intense emotions of grief make life extremely confusing. Grieving adults frequently fear they are losing their minds; how much more so do teens feel the same way. Teens gather their value or self-esteem from others' opinions of them. If their peers do not understand the turmoil during grief, the lack of acceptance of their feelings may cause grievers to bury those feelings, causing more lasting damage.

> *Anger is really the only emotion that I dealt with right away, and probably the emotion I handled the best. The shock just kind of needed time to pass, to be allowed to settle in. I internalized my sadness and remorse entirely. I did not let anyone know how much the loss affected me for over two years. The feelings of loss multiplied greatly due to my internalization of it all. — Chelsea*

Having a support network comprised of caring adults and fellow hurting teens gives them a place to feel, express, and verbalize what is going on inside. It is a big step in the right direction. No one truly understands exactly what they are feeling. Remember, grief is unique, but connecting with others who have also lost loved ones brings comfort. This gives them the affirmation they need that they are not alone, that there are others who "get it" and others who have gotten through it.

One great visual image of emotions is shaking a soda can. If we were to open it quickly after shaking it, we know it would spray everywhere. When we open it slowly, by releasing the pressure with metered control, we can then enjoy the soda without the mess. Grief emotions have similarities to the soda under pressure. There is a choice of either allowing the feelings out a little at a time as they surface or holding them in until they explode—all over themselves and the people they are with. When teens allow themselves to feel and express those feelings as they come, they are less likely to explode later.

Emotions can be overwhelming.

There are times when emotions sneak up on a grieving teen out of nowhere. When grief sneaks up from behind, it can feel like being ambushed. Some people would say it is similar to experiencing an aftershock following an earthquake: it's unexpected. The intense emotions from the ambush can last only a few moments or darken an entire day. It is important to remind them once again that these intense feelings are temporary and healthy to express.

Grief has a multitude of emotions. As their peers and adult friends, part of your job is to share with them which emotions are normal for grief. In this way you can help minimize their anxiety through knowledge.

Not all emotions are felt by every person. Some people revisit the same emotions over and over, while other emotions may never be experienced. One person may have their regrets on auto replay and feel unable to get beyond them, but they may not feel any anger or bitterness. This too is common.

> *The emotions I felt in grief were shock, anxiety, fear, sadness, loneliness (isolated). I cried, mainly at night, because I didn't want to cry in front of people. I prayed. I talked with my family and people who knew and loved my brother John. I wrote in a diary. I wrote about John for school assignments. — Ashley*

Elisabeth Kübler-Ross did groundbreaking work when she wrote *On Death and Dying*.[10] This was the first book to take the emotions felt while facing death, analyze them, and break them into stages. This helped us better understand grief, what is normal and can be expected in death and dying. It was specifically written to describe what she had observed in dying patients.[11] She hoped this would educate doctors, nurses, clergy, and family members about the process of death and dying.

Unfortunately, because it was the first book on the subject of death and dying, it was read by those wanting to know more about grief after the death of their loved ones. The general public came to expect grief to follow Stage 1 through Stage 5—denial, anger, bargaining, depression, and acceptance—in the order Elizabeth had them listed. They assumed that once the anger stage had passed, it would not return and they would move on to the next stage of bargaining. This may have been what she observed in the dying patient, but it does not always hold true for the bereaved.

Grief doesn't follow a pattern. H. Norman Wright describes grief as a tangled ball of emotions with duplicates, several layers, and some emotions being left out entirely.[12] The expression of grief is unique to each person and every relationship. Being unique it follows that the emotions of grief would also be unique. Grief emotions are unpredictable and sometimes can be quite scary, especially for youth. We need to educate ourselves on what is within so-called normal parameters in grief. In educating ourselves as adults and friends walking alongside grieving youth, we are better prepared to bring more comfort to them during the process.

I felt anger, confusion, guilt, depression. I went through just about every kind of emotion I could think of. I couldn't understand it, so I retreated; I hid my emotions pushing everything back into my mind, even my good emotions. – Brian

Emotions of grief are unpredictable.

One moment life is relaxed. For teens this is a time of relief: they can cheer on their football team or enjoy a concert. This is healthy. Unfortunately, outsiders may misunderstand and think because there is laughter the teen is done grieving.

The next moment reality floods in due to a thought, a smell, or a song. The mind flashes on the memory of the friend or loved one who will never be there again to enjoy the laughter with him or her. The emotions ambush them and send the youth crashing quickly to the bottom.

Emotions can stack up.

The youth may feel two or more emotions at the same time: "I am sad over the death of my sister, but I am happy homecoming is tonight." There can be relief over someone who had been battling cancer and no longer has pain; at the same time, there may be deep sadness that he or she is not there to share jokes. This can be confusing, but it is common.

A grieving teen may have linked feelings. He may feel happy while playing basketball, but catching a glimpse of a kid sitting on the sidelines reminds him of his friend who died, so he becomes sad, and the sadness triggers anger over how his friend died; suddenly he is drenched by a tsunami of emotions. These emotions are linked together, overlapping, touching, and all very normal. This is not one feeling after another but feelings on top of each other. Sometimes the teen has no idea where one emotion ended and another began. If you ask where the tears originated, he may not really know.

Think of emotions like the sticks in a game of Pick-Up Sticks. If you ever played Pick-Up Sticks, you can visualize what happens. From a pile of red, blue, green, and yellow sticks, your job is to remove one stick without causing another to move. The first sticks are easy as you pick off the top ones. Eventually you reach the ones that are intertwined, and when one is touched, it moves maybe not one but two or, worse yet, three other sticks. These are like emotions touching one another and triggering new feelings.

Emotions can erupt out of nowhere.

A song that carried no emotion last week opens the flood gates today. The reaction is sparked by thoughts bouncing around unnoticed in the grieving teen's mind. If thoughts of a lost friend were lurking in the background when the song played, the teen's response will be magnified because memories are triggered. Often these thoughts find their own bunny trails scampering from the song to an argument or from a birthday celebration to walks on the beach. The griever has no words to put to where the tears began because the sources are numerous. Bear with your teen in these situations; asking for an explanation can cause frustration. Accept the answer "I don't know" as it is often the honest truth.

- Be present.
- Be patient.

The grieving brain is traveling at warp speed with a flood of emotions that are difficult to sort out. Reality is painful and cannot be escaped. Part of the brain's job is to separate truth from lies by connecting yesterday to today and projecting into the future. Information about a sudden death sends the brain into overdrive searching for the one who is no longer here.

Life as it was does not connect with life as it is now.

This can lead to the feeling of watching one's own life as a third party from the sidelines, detached.

When the brain is so busy trying to connect dots that no longer connect, it strains to concentrate, short-term memory suffers, and absorbing new information is difficult (more on that in Chapter Five).

Denial is one of the brain's ways of slowing down the deluge of painful information. "No, it can't be true" is a common response to the news of a death in the first few days, weeks, and sometimes months. The brain struggles with such devastating information, and it takes time to process the new reality.

Pretending the loved one is visiting friends, away on vacation, or busy with work can be helpful for a time, but the death needs to become real at some point in order to move forward.

To help grieving teens absorb reality, encourage them to do some of the following activities:

- Attend the funeral or memorial service to bring closure.
- Look at photos together and tell stories.
- Retell the story of how they heard about the death.
- Watch the photo video of the loved one's life if one is made.

Some teens want to visit the cemetery or watch a video of the funeral, while others can't bear doing that but will look at photos of their loved ones. Make suggestions but try not to push. It is helpful to know their normal pre-grief personality. This will play into their unique way of processing grief: one teen may need to cry, while another might need to play basketball. One may need to visit the accident scene, while another needs to stay away. Some need to visit the cemetery often, while others can't bring themselves even to consider it. Remember that just like a tattoo, each person's grief is unique to them.

> *Everyone I have told has been completely supportive and very empathetic to how talking about it makes me feel. My closest family and friends knew and were with me when I was at my lowest, but even those I have shared with outside of that circle have been able to relate in some way. — Katie*

Experiencing relief after a loved one's death can be an awkward emotion. In situations where there was suffering and pain, such as an extended illness leading up to death, teens *may* feel relieved the loved one won't suffer any longer. Maybe they are relieved they don't have to be the caregiver anymore but then feel guilty for their relief. Yes, it is common to feel relief; the teen may need your reassurance that this is normal.

Another common emotion associated with grief is shock, which is just what it sounds like: true, physical shock. This is part of early grief. The brain has received an emotionally traumatic hit just as real as a physical trauma. This may manifest as not being able to put two thoughts together. Ask your grieving teens what they need, but don't be surprised if they don't know. Be ready to offer suggestions. This is a good time just to sit with them quietly, allow them to speak if they want to, but mostly just sit. I will talk more about this in Chapter five.

It is during his time of shock that Job's friends in the Bible do a good job: they come and weep with Job, then sit quietly with him for seven days (Job 2:12–13). Job spends chapter 3 grieving verbally. Then, unfortunately, Eliphaz, Zofar, and Bildad blow it. Rather than listen, they open their mouths. For the next several chapters Job's friends attempt to make a case for their belief that Job has brought all his troubles onto himself. When there are no words, silence is the best option. Be present.

It is important for many teens to talk about the death. Discussing the following questions will help bring them closer to accepting their new reality:

- How did they find out about the death?
- What were they told?
- What was their initial reaction?

Verbalizing helps the brain absorb the events, making them real. They need to hear themselves talk it out. Some teens may want their space initially, but eventually they will need to tell their stories, which can be verbal, written, music or drawn as art. Your place is to be available for when they are ready to talk or share the expressions of their stories.

Grief is painful, and they need others to walk with them through it and listen without judgment. As a mentor you will spend a lot of time just hanging out with them and listening. Remember, they think the intense feelings will last "forever".

Society used to suggest that grief was a weakness only girls could express. As the saying went, "Big boys don't cry." Teens need to know that showing grief, mourning, is not a sign of weakness. The reverse of this is thinking that a flood of tears is the only sign of loving deeply. Neither is true. Tears are not needed to have loved deeply, but tears are also not a sign of weakness.

Tears are an expression of emotion God placed in us at creation; otherwise, why did he give us tear ducts? David soaked his couch with tears and Jesus wept at Lazarus's tomb. Neither was a weak man. It is not mentioned in the Bible if Jesus wept upon hearing the death of his cousin— John the Baptist—but I can only assume that he did.

> *I didn't want to be seen as weak or fragile. I didn't want the "It's going to be okay" speech or the "You will see him again" speech.* — *Brian*

The feelings in grief run the entire gamut from anger to relief and everything in between. Here are some activities to help teens put their feelings into words:

- Do an online search using the phrase "emotions of grief." Ask your teen to pick out the emotions he or she is feeling right now.
- Have your teen list the emotions he or she has felt in the last twenty-four hours.
- Mind mapping of emotions is a great exercise; suggest your teen use multiple colors for his or her emotions (I use 'Simple Mind' app on my phone).

The following are some feelings that may be more difficult to deal with.

Guilt

Guilt, according to the *American Heritage Dictionary*, is "the fact of being responsible for the commission of an offense; remorseful awareness of having done some-thing wrong, self-reproach for supposed inadequacy or wrong doing: moral culpability."[13] Guilt implies action for which they had significant responsibility, something the grieving teen believes he or she had purposefully done that led, in this case, to a death.

Regret

Regret, According to the *Oxford Dictionary*, is to "feel sad, repentant or disappointed over something that has happened or been done, especially a missed oppor-tunity."[14] This might happen when the grieving teen wishes he had told his friend not to drive so fast; another may wish she had spent more time at home with or been nicer to her friend at lunch. The "If only" enter in here. "If only I had called her, this wouldn't have happened." "If only I had not asked him to leave." "If only I had told someone what he said." "If only" can haunt teens for a lifetime if it is not dealt with.

Often guilt and regret are confused.

Regrets need to be expressed. It is good to have teens share their regrets with someone they trust, like you. The question you can ask is, "Did you do some-thing on purpose to put them in danger?" If not, then what they feel is likely regret, not guilt. Wishing they had been a better listener is regret. Putting someone in danger on purpose creates guilt, and guilt needs to be worked through with a counselor.

A difficult regret to resolve is when there was an argument shortly before a death. One way to answer this regret is for you to ask your teen, "How were argu-ments resolved with the deceased in the past?" If appro-priate, have them play out the arguments in their heads so they can see their last conflict as resolved. Regret involves circumstances beyond their control.

Anger

Another strong emotion often associated with grief. When there is anger in a grieving teen, seek to better understand whom the anger is directed toward. Maybe he or she is angry with God or at the person who died. Possibly the anger is toward a doctor who may have misdiagnosed or mistreated a disease. Maybe it is toward the driver of the other car or just about the rotten timing of it all. (Why did this need to happen at Christmas?) Anger is a very intense emotion. When a teen exhibits a lot of anger, it may be rooted in deep pain. Extra love, patience, and even sometimes professional counsel are needed. The deep pain needs to be addressed to receive healing.

Here are some ideas of how grieving teens can express anger in a healthy manner:

- punch a pillow or punching bag
- take a run or long walk or bike ride
- go outside and scream or scream into a pillow
- write a letter (but do not mail it!)
- chopping firewood — digging a hole or ditch, if they live in a rural area

Physical activities have an antidepressant effect, and research suggests that it can increase serotonin function, which helps balance mood and calm anger.[15]

I was angry, nothing but angry. I was angry at my dad for being an alcoholic and teaching my brother addictive behaviors. I was angry at my mom for staying with my dad. It took a year after my brother's death before I acknowledged I was angry at him for his bad life choices and drug addictions leading to his death. It was only after that revelation could I begin healing. — Laely

Forgiveness

Another difficult experience that grieving teens may need to face is forgiveness. While dealing with guilt, regret, and anger, there needs to be a discussion about forgiveness. Death complicates situations involving these emotions; it's hard to receive or give forgiveness when teens feel they lost the ability to be heard because their loved one died.

When there is an impression that a loved one's action contributed to the death, forgiveness can be nearly impossible to wrap the mind around. But with God nothing is impossible. Maybe the loved one didn't stop smoking, didn't go to the doctor soon enough, drove too fast, or took his or her own life.

Forgiving deceased loved ones doesn't mean their actions were okay. Forgiveness frees the teen's heart or conscience by not allowing others' actions to have control over him or her. The grieving teen can release the claim to be offended by laying that claim at Jesus' feet.

"I have forgiven in the sight of Christ for your sake,
in order that Satan might not outwit us.
For we are not unaware of his schemes."
— 2 Corinthians 2:10–11

One of Satan's schemes is to paralyze us with bitterness and reluctance to forgive. The responsibility in forgiveness is one-sided, either giving it or receiving it.

When someone apologizes, he or she has no control over whether the apology is accepted by the other person. This applies even more painfully when someone has died. It is important to speak (or write) about the guilt, regret, anger, or action and give an apology. If the infraction is from the deceased loved one, have your teen extend forgiveness to the deceased. "I forgive you for . . . " Then encourage your teen to let it go, knowing he has done his part. This may not be a onetime action but can be repeated when needed.

Sometimes grieving teens feel they need forgiveness from the deceased. Those in heaven cannot carry bitterness. "We become righteous through Christ's atonement."[16] Their sins have all been washed away. Jesus paid the price for all the wrongs they did. They would not hold things from the past against living loved ones. Encourage the teen to accept that forgiveness.

> *"If possible, so far as it depends on you,*
> *be at peace with all men."*
> *— Romans 12:18 (NASB)*

Our responsibility is to live at peace with everyone as much as possible. Clearing our hearts and minds of bitterness is important to moving on with life. Bitterness (not forgiving) harms only the one who holds it. Being bitter is like eating rat poison and thinking it will hurt the other person.

Forgiveness for grieving teens includes forgiving themselves, which can seem even harder sometimes. When teens have the regrets of wishing they "could have," "should have," "would have" done something different, it is a reflection of their need to forgive themselves. God forgives them; therefore, when they do not forgive themselves, they are saying they know more than God. They may need help expressing and grasping forgiveness of themselves.

It can help to have the teens write down what they need to be forgiven for or the forgiveness they want to give. Have them release that paper in some manner like burning it, flushing it down a toilet, or allowing it to wash away in a river or lake. Creating this physical release can help achieve an emotional release.

This process may need to be gone through a number of times before forgiveness is fully resolved. Teens may need professional help if the wounds are deep.

> *It's not your fault; though your relationship wasn't perfect, remember that no relationship is — focus on the good and not the bad — never punish yourself. Remember the love that that person had for you and give it to yourself in their stead. — Mayry*

The healthiest way to walk teens through grief is to encourage them to:

- Feel the feelings and lean into the grief.
- Express those feelings, whether in talking, writing, art, drama, or dance.
- Get plenty of fresh air and exercise and eat healthy foods.

Psychologists agree that these are the first steps in avoiding depression. "Medical studies confirm that depression may often be alleviated and sometimes prevented with good health habits. Eating a healthy diet, getting regular exercise, and taking time out for fun and relaxation, may work together to prevent a depressed mood."[17]

Sometimes teens need to be educated in what is meant by healthy food. Focus on fruit, vegetables, lean meat, and grains, as well as less sugar and less caffeine are good places to start. "Eating a diet that's 70% plant based foods and 30% high quality protein, with healthy fats mixed in, restores energy."[18]

Inviting them to do outdoor activities with you serves two purposes: you connect with them, and they get the fresh air and exercise they need. Even a walk around the mall, park, or neighborhood is helpful. Dancing and other forms of rhythmic movements can also be healing.[19]

Teens need to know you recognize that facing grief is hard work. They have a choice whether to run and hide from their grief or to face it head on and walk through it. Running from grief will not make it go away any more than running toward the sun will keep it from setting. "The quickest way for anyone to reach the sun and the light of day is not to run west, chasing after the setting sun, but to head east, plunging into the darkness until one comes to the sunrise."[20] Leaning into grief, embracing it, and walking through it will hurt, but God has healing and strength waiting for teens when they do.

"Do not fear, for I am with you;
Do not anxiously look about you, for I am your God.
I will strengthen you, surely I will help you,
Surely I will uphold you with my righteous right hand."
—Isaiah 41:10 (NASB)

God knows the amount of reality your grieving teen can deal with at a given time. Do not be surprised if she acts like the death is not affecting her. This may be her way of setting the grief aside, and she needs to know this is okay *for a time*. Or you may need to encourage time away from the grief if your teen seems to be overwhelmed by it. Grief is hard work.

Here is a variety of activities that could provide temporary relief which may be helpful.

- Going to a movie or concert,
- Playing disc golf,
- Playing a video game, and
- Hanging out like "normal" teens.

These are a few ideas that provide a break, something as simple as humming can make a positive difference in mood.[21] Use your imagination.

Grieving teens need to know it is okay to laugh; laughter doesn't dishonor the one who died. If they struggle with this, ask them, "Would the one who died want you to be sad all the time?"

> *"[There is] a time to weep and a time to laugh;*
> *A time to mourn and a time to dance."*
> *— Ecclesiastes 3:4 (NASB)*

Laughter and sorrow are a balancing act. Several months after the death of a loved one, if teens are always happy and never sad, then there is cause for concern that they are in denial or burying the grief. If they are sad all the time without moments of happiness, that too would give cause for concern regarding depression.

Remind teens that the intense feelings are temporary. Despite how they may feel, it will not be this way forever. They will heal and go on to live, love, and laugh — even with a grief-tattooed heart.

You're not alone; though no one will ever experience the loss the way you will, and no one can understand your relationship then or the pain you feel now, people everywhere experience grief.

Let yourself go through the struggle, forgive yourself and others. Allow time to bring healing and teach you. Don't force yourself to deal with the pain in a way you think you "should." – Mayry

Chapter 4 key points:

- They are not going crazy.
- Emotions can't always be anticipated or controlled.
- Intense feelings are temporary; they will go on to live, love, and laugh.

Chapter 5

The Physical Effects of Grief

—ᴟ—

Everything hurts!

"My life is spent with grief, and my years with sighing;
My strength fails because of my iniquity,
And my bones waste away."
Psalm 31:10 (NKJV)

—ɷ—

G rief is not only about emotions, though that is our first thought. God created us with a mind, body, and soul. When one part hurts, so do the others. When we are nervous, we may get stomach butterflies, break out in a sweat, and feel our hearts pound. When we are frightened, our hearts may race. When we receive bad news, we might get sick to our stomachs, throw up, or maybe even pass out. Grief also has a physical side to it, which often is not recognized by grieving teens.

As a mentor try to avoid yes/no questions. Ask open-ended questions using; How, when, what and why:

- How have your sleep habits changed? What is the most difficult to do — going to sleep, staying asleep, getting up, etc.?
- How's your appetite? What food just doesn't sound good?
- How has school changed? How well are you absorbing new information? What distracts you?

With this knowledge you can help them see where grief is affecting them physically. It is good for the school to be aware of the death and that students may be struggling due to their grief.

> *I had very real physical anxiety and depression that included a variety of sensations that could come and go without any predictable pattern that included shortness of breath, heaviness in my chest, waves of sorrow that made it hard to speak/tightening of my throat, body aches, immense fatigue and exhaustion, heaviness/inability to move, stomachache and discomfort, racing heartbeat, quickened or slowed breathing, and weakness. — Mayry*

Many of their aches and pains can be tied back to grief. A stomachache can be experienced especially early in grief, which can diminish appetite. "Anxiety, depression, stress, and grief all express themselves with emotional pain, and quite often gastrointestinal distress."[22] This is to be expected. Recommend that they eat small amounts frequently, but do not push the issue. It is vital that they stay hydrated and do not starve themselves. The other end of the spectrum is nervous eating; especially comfort food like cookies, pizza, and chips. Overeating can lead to other self-esteem issues months down the road. As a friend having input into grieving teens' lives, you can help in directing them toward healthy choices. Their bodies will feel better when they eat well.

> *I felt a weight in my chest that I carried everywhere. I didn't want to eat; I just wanted to sleep. I was always tired, my mind, muscles, eyes; my whole body was always tired. I forced myself to hike or walk around, to paint, something. — Jocelyn*

We speak and even sing of heartache. The heart can physically ache. Suddenly a huge hole or heaviness encompasses the heart with an emptiness that can't be filled. It is a physical feeling of a void left behind by the loved one's death. I do not know the physiological cause of this sensation, but I know it subsides with time. This is the time to affirm that the pain is real, the "hole" they feel is real and is a common experience.

Beth loved putting together puzzles and shopping at garage sales. Two days before her death she found a puzzle at a garage sale: JACKPOT! Quickly the puzzle pieces covered the card table and Beth was focused on its completion.

"Why the rush?" I asked.

"I want to make sure all pieces are here before I put it on the shelf," she replied.

By Monday at noon the puzzle was complete, each and every piece, by 2:00 p.m. she was gone. On Monday evening, friends and family came to bring us comfort upon learning of Beth's and Josh's deaths. The card table containing her puzzle was set off to the side but not disturbed. The next day a dear friend asked if she could build a shadow box for Beth's puzzle. I loved the idea but was shocked to find that just as our life now had a gaping hole, a piece was now missing from Beth's puzzle. We searched but never found that piece.

Part of grief is the realization that an important piece in the puzzle of life is missing. Like in a puzzle, each piece plays an important part in telling the story. When a piece that once was there is now missing, it is difficult to get beyond that hole.

Teens will search for replacement and meaning to the "missing piece." Teens attempt to connect what once was with what is now, and it does not connect; there is a hole because a piece is missing. It takes time to process this missing piece.

In order to process what they are experiencing in life, sleep is vital for teens with or without grief. Usually, according to adults on the outside, the issue is too much sleep. The National Sleep Foundation states that teens need about nine hours of sleep each night to function best; for some, eight and a half hours are enough.[23]

Sleep also might be used as an escape from reality. It needs to be monitored. When grief is raw, sleep may be used as a coping mechanism but after a few months too much sleep can be an indicator of depression.[24]

Insomnia and interrupted sleep is normal *if* it does not last more than three months. The mind is so busy that it keeps a grieving teen awake even if he or she really wants to sleep. A teen who only wants to sleep, can't sleep, or has interrupted sleep for a prolonged period of time may be experiencing depression. In that case, there is need for professional help.

> *I experienced insomnia . . . I got to where I was sleeping maybe three hours a night consistently. I'd catch the occasional full night of sleep and also the occasional night of zero sleep. I didn't realize it was attached to the loss, but as soon as I started actually dealing with the grief and talking things through, it slowly, very slowly, changed. It took a couple years, but I'm back to a normal sleep schedule most of the time now. — Chelsea*

Grief is a stressor

"Stress is your body's way of responding to any kind of demand or threat. Under *stress* your body releases chemicals that give you the added strength and energy you need to protect yourself, but it can also shut down your ability to think, feel and act and your body's ability to repair itself."[25]

"When stress is prolonged, and chronic, it actually breaks down our body's defense mechanism and leaves us vulnerable to disease and illness. You may find that you get colds more often, or you come down with the flu."[26]

The best way to help your teen reduce the stress caused by their grief involves three steps:

1. Getting outside for fresh air.
2. Exercise.
3. Having healthy eating habits.

These serve three purposes: curbing stress, boosting the immune system, and fighting depression.

The death of a loved one is frequently a traumatic loss

Traumatic loss is one that leaves teens feeling as though they just got kicked in the gut and had the rug pulled out from under them. The death blindsided them. If the death came out of nowhere, it is a loss that disables their equilibrium and sends them into a tail spin. They may feel that they are falling, not knowing how far the bottom is beneath them. This is traumatic loss.

"Death is such an assault on the soul. Having someone you love, someone you have shared so much of life with, suddenly yanked from your life is a violent and disorienting experience. Death is so hostile, so explosive to God's design for us, the soul experiences it as trauma. *This wasn't meant to be.*"[27]

In my career as an Emergency Medical Technician, I have seen plenty of physical traumas. I have taken classes over the years in order to keep my skills crisp. To retain my National Registry EMT certification I am required to attend a refresher course every two years. One lecture that caught my attention was on Traumatic Brain Injury (TBI). The lecturer had years of experience with TBI since he was lead physician for the clinic at a major ski area. He saw dozens of head trauma cases each day.

During his talk he listed the symptoms of a traumatic brain injury: headache, nausea, confusion, memory loss, inability to concentrate, difficulty learning and retaining new information. These were symptoms I had experienced while grieving the deaths of my children. I saw those same symptoms in others who lost loved ones traumatically. This began my research regarding the possibility of emotional trauma causing an injury to the brain.

In a physical traumatic brain injury (TBI) a chemical is released stimulating the neurons to reroute around the damaged brain cells and restore normalcy. In an emotional trauma, such as the traumatic death of a close friend or loved one, a similar chemical is released in the brain. It stimulates the neurons to create new pathways around the traumatized region of the brain, the frontal cortex, where memory is stored, in an effort to restore normalcy and make sense of the new reality without the loved one. "In fact, some researchers have likened the effects of traumatic experience to a sort of brain damage."[28]

How do you know if the teen you are mentoring has had a traumatic loss? Regardless of its source, an emotional trauma contains three common elements:

- The event was unexpected.
- The griever was unprepared.
- There was nothing the griever could have done to prevent it from happening.

It is not the event but the individual's experience of the event that determines whether something is emotionally traumatic.[29]

Simply put, those who are grieving a traumatic death have received an injury to the brain. This helps to explain why those grieving may be forgetful, have difficulty learning new things, and be unable to concentrate. It can be as little as losing a set of keys or forgetting what they went downstairs for, not being able to pay attention in class or having no interest in reading the assigned work because they know it won't sink in. It can also be as serious as getting lost while driving in an area of town that is normally very familiar or while driving being emotionally distracted by thoughts and feelings leading to an accident.

The chemistry of the brain is permanently altered, giving rise to problematic behaviors and decreasing ability in certain key areas, learning being one of these key areas.[30] When teens experience a traumatic loss, the inability to absorb new information can cause great frustration unless they understand why it is happening.

Teachers need to be aware of the needs of that teen. Some teens want to be consumed by school. This provides distraction to set aside the grief for a time. Others become bogged down and begin to have difficulty in school. If teachers are able to give focused tutoring or lighten the school load while still keeping the stability of a schedule, this can be helpful. Pushing grieving teens to continue with the same work load as before can lead to failing grades, causing additional emotional distress. These teens are not going crazy, and they are not bad students; their brains are injured. This is temporary.

When grieving teens are forgetful and confused, encourage them to:

- keep lists in their phones or on sticky notes,
- have an up-to-date calendar for assignments and appointments,
- and ask for help.

These are steps to keep them on track. Forgetting something important is just an added stress. Early in grief it may be a good idea to have a responsible friend, who is thinking clearly, drive the teen places. The reason for this is that the confusion levels and emotional distraction can create an unsafe environment.

How long will the physical symptoms of grief last for teens? Let's look at a mild physical traumatic brain injury, a concussion. Doctors have found that what we used to call a simple concussion is truly a more serious condition. A second head trauma too soon after the first has been known to lead to death. The current estimated recovery time for a minor physical concussion is now thought to be six months to a year.

If a physical concussion takes up to a year to recover from, why do we think teens can recover from the emotional trauma of a death in a matter of weeks? Everyone's time line for walking through grief is different. It is damaging to push teens to return back to their old selves too soon. And when there is another death in close succession, it becomes "complicated grief" and requires professional counseling.

Strategies that help to bring about healing for a physical brain injury can be helpful for a grieving brain as well. Give the brain physical rest and cognitive rest:[31]

- Set aside electronics such as cell phones, computers, and video games if using them causes headaches.
- Watch funny old movies.
- Listen to quiet, calming music.
- Use subdued lighting.

Time is an important factor in getting through grief. We have heard the phrase "Time heals all wounds," but this is not entirely true. It is not time that mends a broken bone; a broken bone heals because our bodies are designed to heal. Healing grief takes time too. The healing clock begins not at the funeral but when the teen chooses to lean into and walk through the grief. A teen can walk *around* their grief for a decade and not heal.[32] To walk through grief is a choice that contains several aspects:

- Accept the loss and the reality of what happened. Telling the story is helpful in acceptance.
- Invite God to be a part of it so the Holy Spirit can bring healing.
- Begin to express emotions (journaling, drawing, talking about feelings).
- Be open to accepting a new identity (now the oldest child in a family, a single person, or not dating, etc.).

It also takes time to create new memories to overlay the painful ones. Again, we have all heard "Time heals," but it is not the time that does the healing; it is what happens *during* the time.

In grief, your teen needs to be reminded to be gentle with himself. He has a brain injury. He will not ever return entirely to his old self for a part of his brain has been damaged; repairs are being done. When someone walks with Christ through grief, he or she can become a better person, one who is more compassionate having experienced God's comfort. These are comments I regularly hear from teens who have walked through their grief:

- "I care for people a lot more now."
- "I am a different person. I feel stronger in my power to say good-bye, to feel, and to openly voice my feelings."
- "Coming through it made me more patient, compassionate, loving, genuine, outgoing, ultimately a better person."
- "It drew me closer to the Lord. I had to give him my pain because I couldn't handle it alone."

"In all things God works for the good of those who love him, Who have been called according to his purpose . . . to be conformed to the image of his son." — Romans 8:28–29

God does not cause bad to bring good, but he does take bad things that happen and turn them for good, our good.

Chapter 5 key points:

- Grief can affect teens physically.
- Sleep is vital in processing their grief.
- Traumatic grief can cause an emotional traumatic brain injury.

Chapter 6

Learning Healthy Grief

—◊◊◊—

I will never be the same.

"So you will not grieve like the rest,
who have no hope."
1 Thessalonians 4:13

—ɯ—

Learning healthy grief is an ongoing process. Grieving 101 is not offered as your average college course. Teens learn mostly by example from their families, those they hang out with, the books they read, the videos they play, and the shows they watch. Many teens have experienced considerable grief in their short lives. They may grieve not only over the death of a loved one but also over failed classes, relationship breakups, fractured friendships, and broken families.

Unfortunately, by the time they reach adolescence, grieving teens in today's culture have experienced more loss and seen more death than teens twenty years ago. However, brains mature at the same rate as brains always have. This puts today's teens at a disadvantage.

For comparison's sake, think of the teenage brain as an entertainment center that hasn't been fully hooked up. There are loose wires so that the speaker system isn't working with the DVD player, which in turn hasn't been formatted yet to work with the television. And to top it all off, the remote control hasn't even arrived![33]

Their coping skills as well as the cause and effect portion of their brains, the frontal cortex, are not fully developed until their mid-twenties and for some even later. Like the missing remote control, you can operate without it, but it takes a lot more effort.

We who have experienced loss and have learned to grieve well and live well carry the responsibility to lead teens in learning how to grieve well too. They will grieve not only once but several times in their lifetimes. Each loss is a learning experience built upon their previous losses. When they learn to grieve well, it gives them a good foundation and coping skills for other losses.

When they do not learn to grieve well, one loss is piled onto another loss until the weight is too heavy to carry and the bottom falls out. At this point a counselor is necessary to help them separate the losses and allow healing to happen. Each loss needs to be grieved. Without proper counsel the pile of losses can be overwhelming.

With grief, there are two schools of thought to choose from: Culture and God's. The culture's ways are taught by example as we grow up. Culture does not know if it is right or wrong. It is just the way life is done, by default.

What our culture says about grief:

- Stuff or hide your feelings. As children we are told, "Be brave" and "Big boys don't cry." Buried in these phrases is the message that we are to ignore our feelings, brush ourselves off, and move on.
- Replace what you lost. Usually the first death we experience is the death of a pet. The normal response from the parent is, "Don't cry, we'll get a new puppy soon." In this way we attempt to replace what is lost without taking the time to remember, memorialize, or grieve that loss before moving on.

- Grieve alone. Children are sent to their room to cry. Sometimes this is appropriate, for example, when the tears are a result of discipline. Other times adults just don't want to hear crying. Even as adults we may be told not to bother the grieving because they "need their space" — adult words for "they need to grieve alone."

Some other common questionable phrases during times of loss:

- Time heals. If you just give it time, you will feel better.
- We all live with regrets. There is nothing you can do about it.
- Never trust again. Don't get close to anyone ever again; loss hurts too much.
- There is no complete healing, just "move on" or "pulling yourself up by your bootstraps." (This leaves grief to rear its head years later, often through anger, drugs, depression, etc.)

What God says about grief

The healthy way to grieve is found in the Bible. You can see it lived out in both the Old Testament and the New Testament. When God's instructions are referred to and followed frequently, freedom to grieve and heal will be found.

Trust in the Lord with all your heart
and lean not on your own understanding.
— Proverbs 3:5

- **Feel:** Encourage teens to feel the feelings God gave them. Give them permission to be free to scream, cry, run, ride their bikes, or hit a punching bag. Sometimes they just need to hear that it is okay to express their feelings. Grief is full of emotions, and they need to feel them. Jesus wept and so did King David. Some teens run from their grief and hide in school, busyness, and sometimes drugs or alcohol. Having a relationship with them means being able to see when hiding becomes detrimental to their lives, their relationships, and their ability to grieve.
- **Review the loss:** Help them to face their grief and process it. Be willing to listen as they tell their stories, again and again. Some teens process better on paper or in music, so writing in a journal, drawing, or writing songs about their loss brings healing. Encourage them to hang out in the sad places for a time.
- **Slow down:** Help them to lean into their grief, face it head on, and walk through it. Remind them they are not walking alone and the intense feelings are temporary.
- **Grieve in community:** After a loss they need to be surrounded by supportive community. After Beth's death her girlfriends sought me out. I loved having the interaction with them. We would hug and share Beth stories. I recognized that they needed to be with each other and formed a weekly Bible study focusing on walking through our grief together because we all "got it." Research if there is a teen grief group in your area. Brave Heart, for example, is a camp for those between the ages of ten and eighteen

who have lost loved ones. Information is found at www.campbraveheart.com.

- **Express regrets:** Help them look at their regrets, emptying out the entire box of guilt and regret. Help them to evaluate each "piece" of their regret. Often regret is considered an enemy, the accuser, telling them lies such as "You could have been a better friend" or "You should have called more often." Guide them away from the lies. To continue to replay the regret is living in the past. Encourage them to look at how they were a good friend, the things they did do to help. Encourage them to seek forgiveness, give forgiveness, and accept God's forgiveness. Refer back to chapter four to review the difference between regret and guilt.

- **Keep Christ at the center:** Even when they feel that there is no hope, they need people to come support them. Just being present can remind them of God's faithfulness and love. God cries with them. This might not be embraced early on in grieving. Often when grief is raw, hearing Scripture sounds hollow. The pain may scream so loudly it is difficult to hear God. Give them time and the opportunity to bring up Scripture before you do. Jesus promised he would never leave them or forsake them (Heb. 13:5). He is the only one in life that will always be there even when they don't feel him. He does not die, he does not lie, he can always be trusted, and he will always love them no matter what.

I was thirteen when my friend Jack died suddenly. I was unprepared I had no tools or coping skills. I went to an adult friend. She gave me ideas like singing and writing letters to express what I felt. Overall, those feelings were so intense and overpowering; the best way to deal with them was to feel them. Not to ignore them, run from them, or hide from them, because they would get me no matter where I was. It was just best to feel them in the moment; I would allow myself time to grieve and then move on with my day. — Jocelyn

When families experience a death, friends bring food and spend time with the adults. When teens experience a loved one's death, they need people who will give them a break from the relatives or just sit with them. They are hurting too. Take time to ask how they are really doing and actively listen. Suggest that they hang out with those who "get it" to support one another in grieving in a healthy, healing way. It is healthy for them to listen to one another's stories and have the freedom to talk. Jesus gathered his disciples around him during grief. After hearing of John the Baptists death Jesus said to the disciples, "Come with me by yourselves to a quiet place and get some rest." (Mark 6:31) After Jesus's death the disciples gathered together in the upper room to grieve.

Time does not heal any more than looking at puzzle pieces scattered on a table will somehow put itself together if we look at it long enough. When my son Josh broke his arm, we took him to the doctor who set and cast it. We were given instructions on how to care for his arm while it healed. It is not time that healed his arm but the incredible way God created his body. His bones were hard at work repairing the break. It is not the time that heals a broken heart. It is God at work in that heart.

Your mission is to lead them to God, who created them to receive healing of the heart; he gave us the Holy Spirit, the comforter to bring about his healing for them. In Luke 4:18–19 Jesus clearly states one of his purposes on earth was to bind up, meaning to wrap for healing, the brokenhearted.

Healing does not mean there is no longer any pain. It is when peace and pain can coexist.[34]

They are learning coping skills, and unfortunately, death is a part of life. In life, we will suffer loss. When we learn God's coping skills, we can heal and be better, not bitter.

As a mentor, it is your decision which pattern you will follow and teach by word and example; our culture's way or God's way.

Things you can do to bring comfort to the grieving:

- Acknowledge the loss.
- Give the griever permission to mourn.
- Urge them to talk about the loved one and share stories.
- Offer to share your stories of their loved ones if you have any.
- Offer practical help.
- Keep in touch, especially three, six, nine, and twelve months after the loss and at birthdays and holidays.
- Ask, "How are you really doing?" and take time to listen.

- Compassion is spelled TIME. Spend time sitting, walking, playing basketball, shopping, or drinking coffee — discussing anything they want to discuss.

Our community experienced multiple deaths among their youth. Within three years after the deaths of my three children their friends grieved the deaths of five more students ages 12-18. Two youth died in a car accident, two of accidental drug overdoses, and one died by suicide. Shortly after the fifth, a suicide death of a 14 year old boy, I offered grief support groups for teens in our area. After our ten weeks together I wanted to know what they had learned about themselves in their grief and asked them what they wish they had done differently. Here are some things they shared:

"I wish I would have been more vocal about my feelings."

"Even though I wrote quite a bit, I almost wish I had written more. When I'm having hard days, sometimes it helps to go back and read my words to see how far I've come since that day."

"I wish I had not internalized so much. No matter how awkward or weak I thought I would feel, falling apart and talking about it then would have been well worth it, given how much things escalated as I tried to push it all away."

Each teen learned something different about grief and about himself or herself. With this knowledge they will all be able to grieve in healthier ways after the next loss they experience. I can only pray they experience a lot of life before then.

Things not to do:

- Don't make careless statements. NEVER say, "I understand how you feel," for there is no way you can. If you have grieved the death of a close loved one, you may "get it," but the uniqueness of grief makes it impossible to understand.
- Don't try to explain or answer the "why" question. Having an answer doesn't change the outcome; their loved one is still gone. Listen and acknowledge their pain.
- Don't judge the death in attitude or action. Judgment can be felt even when it is not spoken.
- Don't worry about saying the right words; the only words needed in the early days are "There are no words." Bringing up Scripture before they are ready to hear it can hurt rather than help.
- Don't isolate them or allow them to isolate themselves. Remind them they are not the ones who died. Call, visit, send cards, and include them in activities.

Remind your teens that the intensity of what they are feeling is temporary. They will not feel this way forever. They will heal and go on to live, love, and laugh without the cloud of grief over their heads. If after eighteen to twenty-four months they seem to be backing themselves into a dark hole, please seek professional help. They may be stuck or battling depression and in need of intervention.

Chapter 6 key points:

- Unhealthy grief: tries to hide feelings, replace the loss, grieve alone.
- Healthy grief: feel (lean into the grief), review the loss, slow down, grieve in community, express regrets, keep Christ at the center.
- Peace and pain can coexist.

Chapter 7

Handling Holidays

—*m*—

How can I celebrate?

"Come to Me, all you who labor and are heavy laden,
and I will give you rest."
Matthew 11:28 (NKJV)

—ᴍ—

In the beginning, the tough stuff of grief is each and every moment of each and every day. The things smelled, heard, and seen all bring up strong memories. As time goes on, the sharp edge of grief is dulled, but mementos, keepsakes, pictures, and particular songs or scents can reopen the wound.

During the grief journey there are some days that carry a heavier burden than others and carve a sharper edge into the emotions. Afraid their emotions will overpower them, teens often ignore a quickly approaching birthday or anniversary.

Preparing for those tough days can actually take the power to overwhelm away from the day. Let's take a look at days that may be triggers, especially during the first couple years.

A teen who experienced the death of a family member may find that the days that give them trouble are different from the days that cause trouble for a student who lost a friend. Other teens experience complicated grief after the deaths of both a family member and a friend, so the difficult holidays and anniversaries are many. As a friend walking with grieving teens, strive to be open to their unique needs and circumstances. Try to look ahead to potentially tough days.

Preparing for the tough days is important, and many grievers, teens and adults alike, appreciate others who are willing to help them prepare and walk with them during those days, especially during the first two years. As those tough days approach, take time to picture yourself in their position with their loss.

Imagine the feeling of standing on a moving bus or train. You stabilize your stance to prepare for turns, stops, and starts. You shift your weight in anticipation of the change in momentum. Not preparing for the jerks of the moving vehicle, on the other hand, will catch you by surprise and throw you off balance. It may even throw you to the floor.

Tough days are those turns, stops, and starts on the grief journey. Being unprepared feels like that sudden jolt, tossing grieving teens headlong into intense feelings. In grief, we call those unanticipated turns ambushes or aftershocks. Anticipation lessens the jolt. Teens need to prepare for them or the sudden turns can throw them off balance. Preparation gives them some power in channeling their feelings and gives them options.

Having you there as someone with a clear head is the first step in preparing as they anticipate, plan, and walk through each tough day or season. But you can't be there every moment of every day. Jesus too had experience with grief, and he wants to walk with grieving teens as they face the tough stuff. They may need to be reminded that Jesus is "a Man of sorrows and acquainted with grief" (Isa. 53:3 NKJV).

Two are better than one,
Because they have a good reward for their labor.
For if they fall, one will lift up his companion.
But woe to him who is alone when he falls,
For he has no one to help him up.
— Ecclesiastes 4:9–10 NKJV

Below are some possible triggers and tough days that may be difficult to face depending on the loss. This is not a complete list, but when you can help teens plan ahead, it makes these days easier to deal with. These times are handled best when they feel prepared.

Thanksgiving

The name of this holiday can strike a painful chord. The memories of this holiday can be painful in and of themselves. The thought of the family coming together when there will be at least one empty chair brings pain. The teen's first response may be to avoid it all together.

Apart from the day of Thanksgiving, the underlying pain may be, "What do I have to be thankful for?" Giving thanks is a learned exercise best done daily. When a person is grateful, he or she recognizes God as the source of all that is given. This person is happier, healthier, and enjoyable to be around. There are many benefits of giving thanks, not only to God but to others:

- It takes the focus off of themselves.
- It puts the focus on something positive, emphasizing what they *have* rather than what or whom they *don't have*.
- It raises serotonin levels in the body, increasing happy feelings.

- It boosts the immune system, keeping the body healthy.

It can be extremely hard for teens to give thanks when they are grieving, but being grateful can bring healing. Fostering gratitude can begin with a list of things for which they are thankful. The first time this concept is introduced, you may get push back, so just help them take the first step. Begin with simple things they already have:

- a car to drive, bike to ride, or feet to walk,
- a cell phone to stay connected to friends,
- a house to live in,
- food to eat.

Have them keep their list handy during difficult seasons so they can add to them as other blessings come to mind. Challenge them to write one thing a day they are thankful for and work up to three.

"Appreciation is even more powerful than gratitude. Gratitude is an internal state, whereas appreciation is gratitude expressed outwardly."[35] Appreciation draws people together and by brightening someone else's day they also help themselves. It is a win-win situation. Challenge them to tell one person a day they appreciate them. When you think they can handle it lift the bar and have them not repeat any one for two weeks. Being grateful and showing appreciation will shift their focus off themselves and onto others.

Christmas

The Christmas season used to begin the day following Thanksgiving on Black Friday, but now when stores pack away the pumpkins and spider webs of Halloween, they pull out the trees and holiday lights. It gives no time for a grieving teen to prepare for the emotions that accompany Christmas. This is where you can help. Assist your teen well in advance in evaluating his or her family's holiday traditions by asking the following questions:

- What traditions did your family have prior to the death?
- What traditions do you want to keep?
- What do you want to keep but will need support getting through?
- What traditions do you want to discard, at least for now?
- What traditions need to be put on hold for a year then reevaluated?

Look at the list together and help them make a plan. When the loss was a family member, you have an opportunity to involve the entire family with a plan to survive the holidays. GriefShare has a Surviving the Holidays program with a traditions checklist.[36] Check GriefShare. org to see locations for Surviving the Holidays near you.

Christmas will affect youth differently depending on whom they lost. If a friend died, Christmas may not unearth many memories. But if a family member died, they will be ambushed repeatedly. The pain may assault them from all directions. Grievers of any age may wish to just fall asleep in the middle of November and not wake up until after January first.

For teens who grieve the death of a family member, holidays stink; there is no easy way to say it, and I'm sure they have used more colorful language. For some it is the painful thought that their loved ones are no longer there. For others it is the difficulty watching other families laughing and planning that cuts to the heart. Often it is a little bit of both. Some teens can't identify the source of their pain; it just hurts. Discuss this with your teen; encourage him or her to try to grasp the source of the pain.

When a family member dies, the teen can be triggered by family traditions. The first Christmas after Chris's death was extremely painful especially since he died just after Christmas. As parents we could not bear even to have a tree, much less decorate it. Abby, our only surviving child, couldn't bear to be without a tree, so we compromised: she got a pre-decorated two-foot-tall tree for her bedroom.

As a family, we decided we needed a change of scenery on Christmas Day and planned three days at a ski resort. All of our traditions changed as we attended a local church then opened presents on Christmas Eve and skied on Christmas Day. Agreeing on these temporary alterations to our family traditions drew us together.

Of all the decorations we see year after year, I believe poinsettias are a wonderful decoration for the grieving. They are the only flower I know of that needs darkness in order to bloom. For at least forty days prior to when you want it to bloom it needs thirteen to sixteen hours of complete and uninterrupted darkness daily.[37] It can remind us that beauty can be found in, and come out of, the darkest of times. Candles can remind us that God sent us his light, Jesus, into the darkness. He wants to bring this same light into the darkness of grief.

Christmas is really a griever's holiday for when we set aside the lights, decorations, parties and shopping and look at the real reason for the season is to celebrate Jesus' birth. As we dig a bit deeper the reason for Jesus being born was to die so we may live which is what we celebrate at Easter.

Valentine's Day

In our family Valentine's Day was a special day set aside to celebrate our love for each child. Scott would give gifts to our daughters, Abby and Beth, and I would give gifts to our sons, Josh and Chris. After Josh and Beth died, I was shocked by the emotions when February 14 arrived the first time. I had not prepared and was ambushed; I struggled with how we could celebrate love for our children who were no longer here. We still gathered and shared gifts as a family, and we also bought a family gift to celebrate our love for all the kids.

This holiday can sneak up on grieving teens, especially for those whose girlfriends, boyfriends, or family members have died. It is good to help them plan ahead for what they will do to get through this holiday. The distraction of watching a funny movie, attending a basketball game, or going bowling may be the best antidote for the pain.

Easter

Easter may carry many difficult memories associated with traditions. These traditions need to be evaluated and changed if necessary, at least for a time. You can refer to the steps used to evaluate Christmas traditions.

Easter is a celebration of Jesus. Jesus is the gift God gave to bring his light into the darkness. Jesus's death and resurrection paid the price for our sins and opened the door to heaven (John 10:10). When we have the hope that our loved one is in heaven with Jesus, it brings joy knowing we will one day join them. You can help your teen to have this hope. It comes when they acknowledge everyone has done wrong things in thought word and deed, even them (Rom. 3:23). The Bible calls it sin.

When they do wrong, there is discipline or a penalty. When they speed and are caught, they get a ticket; if they jump off a two-story building, it will probably kill them due to the law of gravity. These are natural consequences for their actions.

There is a penalty for all sin. This penalty was set before the beginning of time. It is a penalty we cannot pay, for it is too large. The penalty is death (Rom. 6:23). Sinners can't pay the penalty for their sins. They need a savior, someone to save them from that penalty (John 14:6).

Jesus already paid that penalty (Rom. 5:8). He died for our sins, but each person individually needs to accept the gift of his payment (Rev. 3:20). By accepting this gift of Jesus's payment for their sins, we have the hope to be joined with our loved ones for eternity (John 1:17).

It is Jesus's payment we celebrate on Easter. When he, a sinless man, paid the penalty for all sin, it broke the bondage death had on all of us. This is why Jesus rose from the grave; death could not hold him (1 Cor. 15:3–6).

When teens accept Jesus's payment, he will walk with them, as he promised, through the ups and downs of life and nothing can separate them from his love (Rom. 8:38). He also assures them of eternity in heaven with him (John 3:16). If they aren't sure that sounds good, then read Chapter Ten on what heaven is like.

Their prayer can be simple: "God, I have sinned. Thank you that Jesus died for those sins. I accept his payment for my sins. Thank you."

Mother's/Father's Day

When a teen has lost a parent, Mother's Day or Father's Day is another tough day. Some call it a Hallmark holiday, just made up to sell cards. He may find it easier just to avoid the holiday and hide away in his room. Or he may need assistance with ideas on how to celebrate all his mother or father was to him. He could buy or make a card, write a poem, paint a picture, light a candle, plant a flower, go fishing, or enjoy his parent's favorite food.

Many people, young and old alike, find it difficult to attend church on Mother's Day or Father's Day because the loss is magnified when the focus of the service is on the special day. It hurts to see others having what they no longer have. Distraction may be the best antidote in the first year.

For parents who have experienced the death of a child, this is a tough day for them as well. It may bring up the question "Am I a good mom/dad?" or "Am I still a mom/dad at all?"

A teen who lost a friend may find it helpful to give a gift to the friend's parent. A phone call, a card, and a text are all welcomed and cherished. Speaking from experience, reaching out this way is a wonderful idea. On my first Mother's Day after Beth's death, four of her friends presented me with sixty-nine roses. (They confessed that they aimed for one hundred but were only able to collect enough money for sixty-nine.) With moist eyes we sat around for an hour telling stories and loving on each other.

Every holiday is what a grieving teen makes it. Without plans holidays can be overwhelming. When you can help your teen put in the effort to make plans to cope in advance, even holidays are easier to get through.

Helping others during a tough holiday can help soften the pain. Working in a soup kitchen serving the homeless can bring perspective. Putting together shoe box gifts for Operation Christmas Child gives your teen someone to give to who is less fortunate than they are. Helping helps.

Chapter 7 key points:

- Tough days differ with each person.
- Making plans in anticipation of the tough day often helps.
- Helping others over a tough holiday can lighten the pain.

Chapter 8

More Tough Stuff

—m—

Where did that come from?

"Here on earth you will have many trials and sorrows.
But take heart, because I have overcome the world."
John 16:33 (NLT)

—ᴍ—

There are tough days apart from holidays. Some of these will be familiar, but others might be surprising. Grief is unique to each teen, but this chapter will discuss days and events that may sneak up on your grieving teen. You can help him or her prepare for the unexpected.

Birthdays

Birthdays are a great time to celebrate the loved one's life. Adrian was fifteen when he died just before Christmas. When his birthday rolled around the next spring, his family and friends wanted to celebrate his life. They gathered at a camp Adrian loved. They wrote notes on balloons, filled them with helium, and released the balloons into the heavens. Through tear-filled eyes they watched until the sky enveloped the colored dots. In their hearts they were sending birthday wishes to Adrian. It was a time of closure and healing. They then gathered around to tell Adrian stories and share cake and ice cream.

Writing letters, releasing doves, or writing notes on balloons to be released are a few ideas of things to do on a birthday to celebrate a loved one's life. Be the one to encourage your teen to get together with friends or family members to exchange stories, play his or her loved one's favorite game, watch a favorite movie, and enjoy his or her loved one's favorite foods. For the teen this may sound extremely difficult to do, but it can be healing for all participants and is well worth the effort and tissues.

Birthdays are good for remembering the joys and adventures of the deceased loved one's life. This is a great time for family friends to write out stories of times with the loved one. Encourage teens to write out everything they remember about the deceased: favorite sports, activities, clothing choices, favorite foods, music, and even what they smelled like.

Documenting remembrances is vital, for memories fade with time. Help your grieving teen seize the memories as they come.

Angelversaries

An angelversary is the anniversary of the date of a loved one's death (day of the month as well as year). I call it their angelversary because in my case it was the day my loved ones met the angels.

Tough days can be monthly or annually. For some the date of death looms dark each month. If the loved one died on the fifth of June, then the fifth of every month can have a dark cloud over it. They might not even be aware of where the cloud comes from, but the subconscious knows.

The three-month, six-month, and nine-month angelversaries after a death can be harder days than expected. Take care to remember these important dates. Show them you remember:

- Call them.
- Drop them a card.
- Take them out for coffee.

This gives them concrete evidence they are not in this alone.

Grieving teens may be more forgetful or moody as these difficult days approach and not understand why. Having others to talk to is important in assuring them they are not going crazy.

Their subconscious and their spirit know it is an angelversary. They may need more space or more friends present depending on their personality. Angelversaries of a loved one's death can be tall hurdles that bring overwhelming feelings.

Here are a few things you might suggest your teen do for an angelversary:

- Light a memory candle.
- Do a balloon release.
- Ask friends to call, text, email,
- Post on the loved one's social media profiles.

Below are some additional days that you might not think would be hard but could be depending on who has died. With this information you can help your teen be prepared for those otherwise unexpected waves of grief.

First or last day of school

For teens who have experienced the death of a peer, the first day of school can be traumatic. Having a plan in place can alleviate some of the emotional ambushes. Here are some common things to have them think through:

- What door will they enter through? Does it matter?
- Where was the friend's locker? Do they want to walk past it or not?
- What classrooms hold the most memories? Are they to be avoided or entered on purpose?
- Do they need to have tissue available?
- What is their planned "escape route" in case their grief gets triggered or emotions become overwhelming?

The first day of school may not sound like it would be a big deal, but for some who have lost a friend, it can be a huge deal. Help them make a plan.

They had left Jack's seat in Spanish and his locker empty for the rest of the school year (he died over spring break). It was hard when we went back to school in August, they had given someone his locker . . . that hurt. I remember some kids wore bracelets and socks that had been made as a tribute. Some kids wore them every day. My mom fought hard to get something in Jack's honor at the eighth grade graduation ceremony. The school agreed to allow a picture of him. — Jocelyn

The last day of school can be tough because it means saying "good bye" yet again as they leave the place they saw their friend the most. This can be especially difficult when the death was during the last year of elementary, middle school or high school. They won't be returning to that building again. The places which hold the strong memories are being left behind. As the mentor, be prepared for them to grieve one more loss.

Special events such as a graduation, wedding, etc.

Special events can be tough when the person who died would have been there for them. A father would have walked her down the aisle or a brother would have been a groomsman. The loved one's presence is missed, and the mind pictures how different it would be if he or she were still alive. You might suggest your teen do something such as a toast at the reception or place an object representing the loved one's presence at the event.

Our daughter Abby experienced the death of all three of her siblings a few years before her wedding. She wanted to do something to acknowledge their importance in her life. She had three tall decorative pillars holding distinctive candles to represent each of her siblings. On the back of the program she gave an explanation. This was her way of including them in her celebration.

New Year's Eve

The first New Year's Eve after a death may overwhelm the griever especially if they stay up till the stroke of mid-night. The brain thinks linearly, therefore subconsciously a grieving teen might expect everyone who had been a part of his or her life in the previous year to move into the next year. When they realize his or her loved one will not enter the new year, it can ambush. Forewarned is forearmed in this case.

Keepsakes

The saying "you can't take it with you" is never so poignant as after the death of a loved one. Those left behind see evidence of their loved ones around every corner in every room. From toothbrushes in the bathroom to snow boots by the back door, all sorts of objects hold memories. Reminders are everywhere, and grieving teens need to sort out what they want to keep and what can be given away.

It is best for big decisions about keepsakes to wait at least a year. If the first impulse is to give away every item that holds the pain of memories, encourage your teen to pack those items up and put them in storage until the rawness of grief subsides. To give items away too soon would likely cause regret when a few months later they realize how much those items meant to them. Waiting is wise.

Because of our individuality and the uniqueness of grief, it takes time to decide what holds deep memories for each person. Family members need to think about what they want to keep, and teens need to be encouraged to make their wishes known since parents can't read their minds.

When Josh and Beth died, Abby was twenty-two and Chris, fourteen. Abby adopted some of her sister's jewelry and a sweatshirt of Josh's. Chris gathered every item of Josh's clothing he could locate and made them his own.

For some teens a sibling's favorite game, a piece of artwork, or a music collection may become precious. This is common and healthy. For others the pain is too sharp and waiting before decisions are made is healthier than jumping to conclusions about throwing away keepsakes. Encourage teens to ask for items that mean a lot to them even if those items need to be packed away for a time. Keepsakes are an important part of the grieving process.

Following Josh's and Beth's deaths, Abby, unknown to us, gathered items that were special to her and put them in a box labeled VIP. These were items that held special memories but she was afraid would be lost in the commotion of life. Six years later she presented this box to us. It contained their baby blankets, Beth's sketch pad, and Josh's army boots, to name a few items. We were able to appreciate and cherish the memories these items brought. After six years these treasures brought smiles rather than tears.

Dreams and nightmares

The subconscious is difficult to understand. Sometimes dreams can be analyzed and some sense can be made of them, but most dreams make no sense at all. Some dreams bring comfort and can be like a friend to grieving teens, filled with a feeling of assurance that loved ones are safe and happy. But dreams may also be like an enemy replaying what teens imagine happened or how they believe they could have changed events.

Some find it helpful to journal their dreams in an effort to understand, while others don't want to remember a dream once they are awake. Be open to what your teen needs. If dreams create fear and anxiety or if they are filled with death and pain, it may be good for your teen to seek counseling.

Mind tricks

Averi's brother Adrian was a track star with legs like a gazelle, breaking school records time after time. After his death Averi vividly pictured him running beside their family car. It brought her comfort feeling he was still with them. The image lasted in her imagination for months, but it slowly dissipated.

Grieving teens may also think they have seen their loved ones. Imagining seeing deceased loved ones at the grocery store, on the football field, or in a parking lot can be either scary or encouraging. Some may call this hallucinating or maybe just wishful thinking. The brain takes a while to sort out truth from lie. This is normal.

Apart from the tough days, grieving teens will face many other ambushes and turns on their journey. When teens prepare for these "turns" in their grief it takes away some of their power to surprise the teens. When the doctor prepares us for a shot or a tattoo artist begins his art, the recipient is warned so that hopefully he or she won't jump. Knowing what may be coming does not eliminate the pain, but it takes the surprise out of it.

It may be a smell or sound that brings back a flood of memories. Sometimes the flood is followed by sadness, tears, or anger. The suddenness of the feelings can be overwhelming. This is very common. Remind teens they are not going crazy. They are not stuck in their grief just because they want the world to just go away or because they burst into tears for no reason they can explain. The ambush is temporary.

Additional losses

We all have dreams of how we imagine our milestones will be. Anticipated milestones include college graduation, wedding, births of children, and the legacy we will leave behind. Teens have just begun to consider what milestones their lives may hold.

Teens also use today as a template for tomorrow. If they are happily dating today, then they assume tomorrow they will still be happily dating. Likewise, the friend who went dirt biking or shopping with them today will be there to celebrate their high school graduation in the future.

When a death crashes into their reality, it steals not only from their today but from their tomorrow as well. As they reach milestones in their lives, they are again faced with the reality that their loved one is no longer here.

- Summer arrives, but your teen's friend is not there to hang out with.
- Your teen graduates, but his or her parent or friend is not there to celebrate.
- Your teen later gets married and has his or her first child, but Mom or Dad is not there.

Each milestone carries with it the reality of the loss and the death of yet another dream. The grief over these additional losses needs to be expressed. This is a part of grief that is not over in a year or two but can extend over their entire lives. This is where the grief tattoo on the heart shows its permanence.

Each additional loss needs to be grieved. Tears falling years after the death does not mean your teen is stuck in grief: it may mean that he or she still has additional losses to grieve.

Walking with a grieving teen during the tough stuff and the hardest of days can be challenging, but it is worth the effort, and you may be his or her only companion. If not you, then who?

Each milestone carries with it the reality of the loss and the death of yet another dream.

Chapter 8 key points:

- Make a plan for the tough days.
- Share memories, as memories fade unless they are documented.

- Grieving teens need to take time to remember their loved ones.
- Encourage them to be thankful for the amount of time their loved ones were here.

Chapter 9

Why Is There Suffering?

—m—

Why did this happen?

"For we are not fighting against
flesh-and-blood enemies,
but against evil rulers
and authorities of the unseen world,
against mighty powers in this dark world,
and against evil spirits in the heavenly places."
Ephesians 6:12 (NLT)

Talking about why there is suffering is a difficult and sometimes touchy subject. Unfortunately, many people see suffering as *always* coming from God, therefore justifying being angry at God. The other perspective is seeing suffering as *always* being inflicted by the devil: "The devil made me do it." Because neither of these perspectives is accurate, I want to address four primary causes of suffering in this world. Knowing these causes can help you in answering some of the "why" questions you may hear from grieving teens.

The overarching reason for suffering is we are broken people who live in a broken world.

The first two causes of suffering deal with the cause and effect of our actions. When we recognize that our actions and the actions of others can be the cause of suffering, answering the question of why something happened becomes simpler, though not any easier.

The second two causes of suffering point to the struggle between spiritual forces. We are caught in the middle of a spiritual battle of good and evil. We recognize this battle as our box office hits pit good against evil: Star Wars Resistance fighters battle the Empire;

Frodo in Lord of the Rings has to protect the ring from Sauron; Harry Potter battles against Lord Voldemort.

When a teen can view his or her suffering through the lens of "God, what can I get out of this?" rather than "God, get me out of this," it can lead to deeper maturity. In life we often want the easiest route around a problem. Sometimes God knows we can be strengthened by working through a problem. When we face a mountain of troubles, it may be best to ask God for the strength to climb it instead of wanting him to remove it. The familiar saying seen in fitness gyms states, "No pain, no gain." The same can apply in life though we hate to admit it.

Listed below are four causes of suffering:

1. Suffering caused by our own errors and poor decisions

We can be the cause of our own suffering. This can be as simple as choosing to carry a cell phone in a jacket pocket, then forgetfully tossing the same jacket into the laundry. I say this from experience: When a teen chooses not to study for an exam and then fails, he or she will suffer the consequences. The suffering can be as devastating as getting arrested, injured, or possibly even death after choosing to drive drunk. Unfortunately, suffering brought on by our decisions or actions rarely affects only us.

2. Suffering caused by the decisions and actions of others

This kind of suffering is multiplied just like ripples from a pebble dropped in a pond. For those affected it may feel more like a tsunami caused by an earthquake when we suffer from another's actions. Having someone to blame rarely makes anything better, and the answer to "Why?" will continually elude us. Legal action, whether taken by the courts or filed by the one wronged, tends to drag out and complicate the grieving process. Each court date reopens the wound, delaying the healing.

The healthiest way to deal with the pain when suffering is caused by someone else is to grieve the loss, then forgive the person at fault. Yes, it is easier said than done, but as long as there is sin, forgiveness needs to be part of life. Forgiveness will not be a onetime event but may need to be given each time the pain from the offense comes to mind.

When the offender has died, forgiveness gets complicated. The teen may be used to forgiving only when an offender repents. When the offender dies, the opportunity to repent in person is removed, but forgiveness can still be given. The grieving teen is only responsible for forgiving. Jesus doesn't say forgive if the person repents; he says to forgive as we are forgiven.

When a loved one's action contributed to his or her death, forgiveness is difficult and seems impossible to wrap the mind around. He or she didn't stop smoking, didn't go to the doctor soon enough, was texting while driving, was driving too fast for conditions, or maybe took his or her own life. Regardless, the truth is that unforgiveness holds us in bondage.

Forgiveness doesn't mean the action was okay, but it is the freeing of the teen's own heart or conscience. He or she releases his or her claim to be offended.

> *"If it is possible, as far as it depends on you,*
> *live at peace with everyone." Romans 12:18*

The grieving teen is not responsible for the other person and whether he or she accepts forgiveness. The grieving teen is only responsible for his or her own action of forgiveness.

3. Suffering caused by living in a fallen world

In life we have an Enemy. His name is Satan. Satan hates God, really hates him. We were created in God's image. "God created man in His own image" according to Genesis 1:27 (NASB). Therefore, Satan hates us and strives to do us harm in any way he can. Think back to the Garden of Eden. Satan lied to Eve, and she was deceived into eating the fruit God had forbidden her and Adam to eat. She invited Adam to join her, and just as God warned them, their actions brought death. God and Satan both have an agenda. God's agenda is to bring life Satan's agenda is to bring death. Satan was the root cause of death from the very beginning.

If we contrast the character of Satan to the character of Jesus, we can see much of the source of suffering:

Satan	Jesus
Hates	Loves
Kills (John 8:44)	Heals (Acts 9:34)
Steals (John 10:10)	Encourages (Ps. 10:17)
Destroys (John 10:10)	Brings life (John 10:10)
Lies (John 8:44)	Speaks truth (John 14:6)
Accuses (Rev. 12:10)	Forgives (Luke 7:49)

When teens are grieving, what does Satan want them to do? He wants them to blame God and take it out on God when Satan is really the one to blame. After the death of a loved one, teens may be angry. There likely will be a crisis of faith. This is very normal. They need to analyze the cause of the death and decide whom the anger should be directed toward. This is difficult to do, and there may be more than one cause.

Helping teens grasp that they have an enemy named Satan will often help answer the question of "Why is there suffering?" Satan knows God loves his children, and when he inflicts pain on them, it hurts God. I believe strongly that when teens cry, God cries with them. The difference is God sees the other side of the coin, for *"If God is for us, who can be against us?" (Rom. 8:31).* When Satan intends evil, God brings good.

Deadly and terminal illnesses like cystic fibrosis, spinal meningitis, and cancer would fall into this category of evil ultimately caused by Satan. Living in a fallen world is the root cause of the disease we suffer. No matter what was the cause of the death of your teen's loved one, Jesus— the God of all comfort (2 Cor. 1:4)—wants to bring his child comfort and peace.

4. Suffering caused by the hand of God

"For the Scripture says to Pharaoh,
'For this very purpose I have raised you up, that I might
show my power in you, and that my name might be
proclaimed in all the earth."
— Romans 9:17 (ESV)

The Israelites were slaves of Pharaoh, but God intended to set them free. God through Moses brought many sorrows and calamities upon the Egyptian people. God caused sorrow to convince Pharaoh to release the Israelites. The parting of the Red Sea opened the way for the Israelites to escape. The parting of the Red Sea brought death to many Egyptians but freedom to the Israelites. If pharaoh had not had such a hard heart there would have not been so much suffering (Exodus 7-14).

In John 9:2-3 Jesus' disciples asked him,

> *"Why was this man born blind? Was it because
> of his own sins or his parents' sins?"*
> *"It was not because of his sins or his parents'
> sins," Jesus answered. "This happened so the power
> of God could be seen in him.*
> *Then he spit on the ground, made mud with the
> saliva, and spread the mud over the blind man's eyes.
> He told him,*
> *"Go wash yourself in the pool of Siloam" (Siloam
> means "sent").*
> *So the man went and washed and came back
> seeing! (NLT)*

No one was at fault for this man's blindness. To bring God glory and draw men closer to him through his healing was the only reason for this man being born blind

Hurricanes, tornadoes, floods, forest fires, and other natural disasters have all been attributed to "the hand of God." They have devastating effects on people caught in their paths, but God does not cause them. They are normal occurrences we experience living on this fallen planet. Knowing that, however, does not make it any easier when a loved one dies.

I spent an afternoon once on a mountain top overlooking a twisty road. I watched as someone made a poor judgment call and passed another car on a curve. If he had collided with an oncoming car, would I have been the cause since I was a witness? No, we understand that merely observing an incident as it unfolds does not cause it to happen. God sees us as we make bad judgment calls. He is with us when everything in life goes awry. Just because he sees doesn't mean he is the cause.

God isn't limited by time or space. He has already seen what will happen. He has watched us as we make bad decisions and good ones.

Often people throw around Romans 8:28: *"in all things God works for the good of those who love him, who have been called according to his purpose."* The question that verse may leave you with is what does God mean by "good?" When you read further, you see God's definition of good in verse 29: *"For those God foreknew he also predestined to be conformed to the image of his Son"* This helped me understand that becoming more like Christ is what God sees as the "good" that can come out of suffering.

When an artist begins to sculpt, he takes a block of material and pictures the end result. If the end result he desires is a bugling elk, he will begin to chip away all that doesn't look like a bugling elk. God sees us as he created us to be and allows "all things" to chip away at everything that doesn't fit. Sometimes we don't know the piece of art God is creating in us.

No one wants to suffer, but everyone will. It is not the suffering itself that brings maturity, but it is what is done with the suffering. You can help teens when they hit the bottom. Rather than looking down into the mud and having a pity party, with your encouragement they can look up and take hold of God's hand and allow him to strengthen them.

> *I waited patiently for the Lord;*
> *he turned to me and heard my cry.*
> *He lifted me out of the slimy pit,*
> *out of the mud and mire;*
> *he set my feet on a rock,*
> *and gave me a firm place to stand.*
> *— Psalms 40:1–2*

Your job is to show these teens the healthiest way to deal with suffering, which is turning to God for comfort and strength.

Satan wants grieving teens to stay focused on the tragic events in their lives. God knows tragedy brings suffering, and he will comfort them in it. Ultimately, God wants these teens to focus on how they can help others, for helping helps. They can bring others comfort because of the comfort they received in their suffering (see 2 Cor. 1:4). You can be the tool God uses to bring that comfort as you walk alongside them.

Satan meant Jesus's death to be the end of God's plan, but he failed to recognize it was just the beginning. Without Jesus shedding his blood on the cross, there would be no forgiveness for sins and no resurrection to open the door to eternal life.

Even when things look darkest, God is leading the way and showing us *"the treasures of darkness and riches from secret places' (Isa. 45:3 HCSB)*. Sometimes part of the treasure is a closer walk with God or a more compassionate spirit.

In nature, there are two distinct examples of beauty coming out of the darkness. As I described in chapter seven, the poinsettia plant, which is sold during the Christmas season, has to be forced to bloom by putting it in darkness. The flower is unique and beautiful, refreshing in the midst of the cold and barren winter season.

The second example is the pearl. A pearl begins to form when a grain of sand gets into an oyster shell. The sand causes pain. The oyster releases a chemical to cover over the sand to eliminate the discomfort. This cycle repeats itself until the oyster dies. Only then can the pearl be harvested. The precious pearl comes out of pain and death, just as the beautiful poinsettia blooms because of darkness.

The list of beautiful things coming out of darkness and death is long. Here are just a few examples:

- MADD, Mothers Against Drunk Drivers, was formed because a child was killed by a drunk driver.
- Michael J. Fox has put a face to Parkinson's disease, and great strides have been made toward curing that disease because of him.
- Joni Erickson Tada became a quadriplegic after a diving accident when she was seventeen. After a battle with depression she started several ministries for people with disabilities. She also wrote a multitude of books that have been read by millions.
- Nancy G. Brinker promised her dying sister, Susan G. Komen, that she would do everything in her power to end breast cancer forever and later founded Susan G. Komen for the Cure.

If God is for us, who can be against us.
— Romans 8:31

Chapter 9 key points:

- Suffering has four causes: our decisions, others' decisions, the spiritual battle between good and evil, and natural causes.
- Ask God, "What can I get out of this?" rather than "God, get me out of this."
- In all things God works for the good of those who love him.
- Beautiful things can come out of darkness.

Chapter 10

Heaven

—⁓—

I can only imagine.

"In My Father's house are many mansions;
if it were not so, I would have told you.
I go to prepare a place for you."
John 14:1–2 (NKJV)

E ach of us has an internal longing: a longing for something more, something heavenly, when we die. Few of us have any idea what that really means. As Christians we long for heaven, but when we, as adults, dig back into our mental archives and try to explain a place as magnificent as heaven must be, our descriptions can seem very nebulous and indistinct.

MercyMe asks us what we think will happen when we enter Heaven in their song "I Can Only Imagine." The song questions the types of responses we will have once we are face to face with God, but they are responses we can "only imagine". In our hearts we just know it will be beyond our current knowledge.

One night as my seventeen-year-old daughter Beth was heading off to bed, she asked me, "What is heaven like? I know all about the streets of gold and the gates made of a huge pearl. What else can you tell me?" I really didn't have anything to add to what she already knew. I had not studied heaven at all, and my ignorance showed. Unlike all the energy and time I had put into planning our last summer vacation, I had put no effort into learning about my final destination where I will spend eternity.

When Beth died three months later, it set a fire inside me to learn all I could about heaven. Can we even imagine what waits for us there? According to 1 Corinthians 2:9–10, *"Eye has not seen, nor ear heard, nor have entered into the heart of man the things which God has prepared for those who love Him"* (NKJV). According to Revelations 21:1–4, this old earth goes away and we get a new heaven and a new awesome earth where there will be no more death or mourning or pain or crying and Jesus will wipe away all our tears. This sounds pretty incredible to me.

Since Beth's death I have read many books about heaven, including *90 Minutes in Heaven: A True Story of Death and Life* (by Don Piper with Cecil Murphey)[38] and *Heaven is for Real: A Little Boy's Astounding Story of His Trip to Heaven and Back (by Todd Burpo).*[39] These were good but I wanted information I could sink my teeth into. Then I found Randy Alcorn's book *Heaven*[40]. It was loaded with great Bible-based information.

Randy spent twenty-five years researching the Old and New Testaments before penning what he had learned. Most of the information contained in this chapter I gleaned from the scriptures he cites in his book. It is time we learned what we can expect in heaven so we can pass this information on to our youth.

Youth have a smaller scope of life experiences to draw from, so defining heaven may be even more difficult for them. We use expressions like "these are heavenly," "heaven on earth," or "a taste of heaven," but we are limited because we have only earthly experiences for comparisons.

Walking on Clearwater Beach in Florida I was amazed at how soft the sand was. I tried to describe it to a friend but came up very short. Maybe it was as soft as deep velvet, but that was not quite it for it filtered between my toes. Maybe it was like walking through flour, no that was an incomplete description. Each step felt heavenly. There was nothing for me to compare it to this side of heaven.

God wants us to be able to picture heaven, but in our limited imagination we can't see it. In Revelation 4:3 John uses comparison to describe what he sees: *"And the one who sat there had the appearance of jasper and ruby. A rainbow that shone like an emerald encircled the throne."* He had seen nothing like it on earth but uses jewels to convey the depth and brilliance of colors. The word "like" is used fifty times in Revelation, emphasizing John's struggle to describe what was revealed to him by God. "God has given us glimpses of Heaven in the Bible — to fire up our imagination and kindle a desire for Heaven in our hearts."[41]

For our last family vacation before Abby left for college, we took a road trip to South Padre Island. I spent weeks planning out every highway, major meal stop, and overnight accommodation. The younger kids, Beth and Chris, studied Texas history, food, and culture. They knew what weather to expect and the activities they wanted to do when they arrived. Chris, our youngest, then age ten, wanted badly to fish in the ocean. He hid a collapsible pole and tackle box under the van seat and produced it upon our arrival. He pictured it, planned it, and then presented us with a three-pound flounder he caught off the pier. The planning that goes into a vacation can take months and contain a multitude of details, raising everyone's anticipation of the vacation.

What comes to mind when you try to picture heaven? Do you see big puffy clouds where we all become angels and sit around strumming our harps like the cartoons portray? Maybe you think it will be like church for eternity. Honestly that doesn't sound like fun to me. I really love our church's worship nights. It may extend for even a couple incredible hours, but eventually I feel a need to go home. If heaven were like that, I am not sure I could look forward to being there forever.

Jesus said heaven is like a mustard seed; it is the smallest of seeds but grows into a tree the birds build their nests in (Matt. 13:31). With that comparison I would say our concept of heaven is as small as a mustard seed in comparison to what it really holds. Getting even a small glimpse of heaven can change the whole landscape of our lives and how we live it. I want to help you expand your knowledge of heaven so you can share it with the grieving teen in your life.

Because God wants us to know more about heaven, he let John see a glimpse of what it is like, and then John documented what he saw in the book of Revelation. The most well-known description of heaven is found in Revelation 21:21: *"The twelve gates were twelve pearls, each gate made of a single pearl. The great street of the city was of gold, as pure as transparent glass."* Most of us have heard this yet fail to realize that, as awesome as it sounds, it is just the beginning.

Revelation 6:9–10 takes us deeper: *"When [the lamb] opened the fifth seal, I saw under the altar the souls of those who had been slain because of the word of God and the testimony they had maintained. They called out in a loud voice, 'How long, Sovereign Lord, holy and true, until you judge the inhabitants of the earth and avenge our blood?'"* The saints' statement in and of itself sounds pretty depressing, but these verses give us a lot of information about heaven and the future:

- **We will know Christ and recognize him as judge.** The saints "called out, 'Sovereign Lord, holy and true, how long until you judge?'"[42]
- **There is a marking of time.** They wonder "how long?" but time will work not against us but for us. We will never "run out of time" or need to fear that there "won't be time," for we will have an eternity.[43]
- **The souls asked a question.** This verse reveals we will not know everything, but we will know more clearly and continue learning. Our learning may be as different as watching a show on a black-and-white TV and then watching it in HD. The show is the same, but there is greater clarity. I think learning will come easily, and we will be hungry to learn more, exponentially adding to what we learned while on earth.

The rest of the Bible uncovers details of heaven that we can add to our picture:

We will know our loved ones.

We will be remembered for our testimony on earth, for even now we are *"surrounded by such a great cloud of witnesses" (Heb. 12:1)*.[44]

We will see what is happening on earth

We will see events that are taking place on earth. Imagine taking a two-year-old child for a walk and stopping to show her a spider web glistening with dew. You pause and look into the world of that spider for just a moment. Similarly God allows the saints to catch glimpses of happenings on earth. (1 Samuel 28:16-19)

"Those on earth may be ignorant of Heaven, but those in Heaven are not ignorant of Earth."[45]

We do not become angels.

Death is a relocation of the same person to another place. The place changes, but the person does not. After Jesus rose from the dead, he walked with two men on the way to Emmaus (Luke 24:15). When they arrived, they invited Jesus to stay and share a meal (Luke 24:29). Jesus was still a person who ate, drank, and walked — he had not become an angel: *"we know that when Christ appears, we shall be like him"* *(1 John 3:2)*.[46]

Heaven is full of adventure

"Our days on earth are but a shadow" *(Job 8:9)*. As Paul describes time and the future, *"For now we see only a reflection as in a mirror; then we shall see face to face"* *(1 Cor. 13:12)*. It took God six days to create earth, but Jesus has been preparing heaven for us for over two thousand years (John 14:2). When God reveals the new heaven and new earth, it will blow our minds. God created us with a desire for adventure, although admittedly he put more desire in some people than in others.

There are trees and rivers and animals in heaven.

The River of Life will run through the new Jerusalem. *"Then the angel showed me the river of the water of life, as clear as crystal, flowing from the throne of God and of the Lamb down the middle of the great street of the city. On each side of the river stood the tree of life, bearing twelve crops of fruit, yielding its fruit every month. And the leaves of the tree are for the healing of the nations"* *(Rev. 22:1–2)*.

There are also horses because Jesus comes to earth riding a white stallion: *"The armies of heaven were following him, riding on white horses and dressed in fine linen, white and clean" (Rev. 19:14). "The wolf will live with the lamb, the leopard will lie down with the goat, the calf and the lion and the yearling together; and a little child will lead them" (Isa. 11:6).* For me, if there are horses, wolves, lambs, leopards, calves, and lions in heaven, then our beloved pets should be there too.[47]

There will be everything we desire but can't find on earth

In heaven, there is no pain, no tears of sadness, no suffering, and no death. Heaven is safe, a place of ultimate peace. Knowing our loved ones are in heaven having their own adventures is a great comfort. For those who have accepted God's free gift of Jesus's payment for their sins, there is hope, not hope like "I hope I get an iPad for Christmas" or "I hope I pass my physics exam" but an assurance we will be spending eternity with those we love having adventures in heaven together. We have loved ones who have gone on ahead of us. They are absent from the body but present with the Lord.

God has purpose in us still being here. Youth need to know they have purpose, especially after the death of a loved one. Finding a place where they can volunteer is a great beginning. Here are some ideas to suggest to your grieving teen:

- Go on a mission trip.
- Feed the hungry at a downtown meal kitchen.
- Pack shoeboxes for Operation Christmas Child.
- Work with Samaritan's Purse in disaster relief.

- Visit the elderly in a nursing home.
- Write and record a song

We have received comfort so we can comfort others with the comfort we received (2 Cor. 1:5-6). Helping helps. Grieving teens have a choice: have the trials and grief turn into bitterness, souring the rest of their lives, or allow the trials and grief to mold them into kinder, more compassionate and loving people. They need to be made aware of this choice. Bitter or better?

Teens often believe the feelings they have today will last forever. They need to have it brought to their attention that this too shall pass. Feelings are temporary. Trials on earth may only make sense from heaven. *"For our light and momentary troubles are achieving for us an eternal glory that far outweighs them all"* (2 Cor. 4:17). *"Blessed is the one who perseveres under trial because, having stood the test, that person will receive the crown of life that the Lord has promised to those who love him"* (James 1:12).

But there is one thing we can do here we can't do in heaven. We cannot share God's love with those who don't know Christ. That has to be done here. All of us, no matter what age, have work to do while we are here. *"We are God's handiwork, created in Christ Jesus to do good works which God prepared in advance for us to do"* (Eph. 2:10). God would likely say to us what he said to Jeremiah; *"Do not say, 'I am too young.' You must go to everyone I send you to and say whatever I command you"* (Jer. 1:7).

God wants to walk with the grieving; no matter what their age, they need to hear about Christ's love. He desires to wipe every tear. He wants to carry them through the valley of the shadow of death. We can be Jesus's hands and feet, and *"How beautiful are the feet of those who bring good news!"* (Rom. 10:15). When we walk with the grieving, we have the opportunity to tell them of Jesus's great love and his desire to walk with them too. He is the man of sorrows acquainted with grief. He gets it!

We can only be with someone part of the time, but Jesus is available all of the time, every hour of every day, even at 2:00 a.m., but Jesus is a gentleman and waits until he is asked.

Often teens and adults are blind to what God has in store for them in heaven and on the new earth. It is worthwhile exploring and setting our eyes on what is yet to come, what is unseen. In doing so, we are freed from the "bucket lists" of this life, such as seeing the seven wonders of the world or visiting all the National Parks before the end of our lives. We will have an eternity to explore a new untarnished earth. That frees us to do the work God has given us to do while on earth.

We all will have to wait until we reach heaven to hear about all the adventures our loved ones have had while they waited for us.

Now is our time to plan for eternity.

Chapter 10 key points:

- We will all spend eternity somewhere; to make no decision is to decide against heaven.
- God has purpose in your grieving teen still being here.
- Heaven is better than his or her wildest imagination.
- Jesus "gets it."

Conclusion

—⁓—

—ᨒ—

You are the one who can make a difference in the lives of youth impacted by loss. You are Christ's hands and feet. You now have the tools to show them there is light and hope even in the darkness of loss.

When Chelsea called two years after my son Chris' death she was very candid with me.

"Chris's death is affecting me more deeply than I thought it would or even should." She began, "Sure we were in Chemistry together, but we weren't close." She paused. "The only people around me who died were, well, older. Chris' death has been really difficult."

"Would you like to get together and talk?" I questioned, hoping she would take me up on the offer.

"Are you sure?" she asked, 'Yes, I think I'd like that. I haven't talked to many people about it because I feel like it is silly for me to hurt so much."

We began meeting regularly over coffee or breakfast. We slowly uncovered her grief tattoo revealing struggles in her life connected to her grief. She was relieved to realize she was not going crazy. She was grieving. Discussing the uniqueness of her grief helped her to relax with the knowledge that the things she was experiencing were very common.

Using H. Norman Wright's tangled ball of grief discussed in Chapter Four we explored the varied emotions that she was experiencing in her grief. With so many facets of her loss she didn't realize how feelings could stack, repeat, or never surface. Once this was revealed she became more at peace.

The physical aspects of grief intrigued her. This answered her question of why she struggled with sleep and was easily irritated with little tolerance for, in her words, "petty things." When we discussed the emotional trauma her brain experienced due to Chris' suicide she gained a new understanding of her forgetfulness and inability to absorb new material.

As our meetings continued, Chris' birthday approached, followed by the holiday season. It was good to open the box regarding how she could deal with these difficult days better. We planned ways to celebrate his life on his birthday. We took a close look at what traditions needed to change. If any. No sooner had Christmas passed, and then it was Chris' angelversary. Each of those tough days cast their own shadow. We laid out plans to distribute the emotional load over a few days prior.

Chelsea breathed a sigh of relief. She had struggled with all this alone due to her own isolation. Now someone was here to share the burden and lighten her load. Now that she had a loose handle on the uniqueness, emotions, physical aspects, and how to handle the tough days, other questions arose.

"Why is there suffering anyway?" Chelsea asked.

I knew this question had been hiding in the shadows and was glad she finally asked. Eventually the subject of why there is suffering is often broached. Everyone asks that question whether silently in prayer or boldly out loud even if we may not expect an answer.

When this subject surfaced we explored each of the four possibilities. With Chris she knew that her suffering was brought on by his spontaneous bad decision. There were many other times she experienced suffering and discussing the root of suffering brought her to a better understanding as a whole.

Facing death at such a young age brought forward the question of "What happens next?" followed closely by "What is heaven like?" Taking time to explore these questions brought her peace of mind knowing that even though Chris took his own life he knew Christ as his savior and that opened the doors of Heaven when the time came.

Chelsea began to relax and happiness became a part of her life again.

One day she asked, "Would you mind meeting with a friend of mine? She has experienced many losses. I think you could help her."

"Of course, I'd be happy to talk to her." I replied.

"Good because I already gave Stephanie your number." Chelsea responded, "She's expecting your call."

I put Stephanie's number into my phone, and the next day I called and we set up our first meeting.

At lunch a few days later I listened to her story and answered a few questions. The conversation came to a natural pause before Stephanie stated, "Now I know where Chelsea gets her information."

Stephanie said in a matter of fact tone, "She has been a great help during this tough time."

Chelsea had taken what we discussed and passed it on to Stephanie. In doing so, Chelsea became a grief mentor.

You now have the tools to help your teen to uncover their grief and bring it into the light. It is in the light that they will be able to see it for what it really is a natural response to an un-natural event.

When God created us there was no death. We were not created for such deep sorrow which is why when we grieve God grieves with us. We have a need to live in community and grieve in community. You, as their mentor, become a vital part of that community.

Tattooed by Grief was written for this purpose, for you to gather the tools you need for helping youth around you who have been impacted by loss. You never know when they will take what you taught them and use it, just like Chelsea sharing her new knowledge with Stephanie and the two sharing it with their friends.

This is where you come in.

Starfish Story

Original story by Loren Eiseley[48]

—∿—

One day a man was walking along the beach when he noticed a boy picking something up and gently throwing it into the ocean. Approaching the boy, he asked, "What are you doing?"

The youth replied, "Throwing starfish back into the ocean. The surf is up and the tide is going out. If I don't throw them back, they'll die."

"Son," the man said, "don't you realize there are miles and miles of beach and hundreds of starfish? You can't make a difference!" After listening politely, the boy bent down, picked up another starfish, and threw it back into the surf.

Then, smiling at the man he said, "I made a difference for that one."

Endnotes

—ɯɯ—

Introduction

[1]   "204 School Shootings in America Since 2013," *EverytownResearch.org*, accessed November 19, 2016, https://everytownresearch.org/school-shootings/.

[2]   "Basic Facts About Teen Crashes," *TeenDriverSource. org*, accessed July 14, 2016, http://www.teendriver-source.org/stats/support_teens/detail/57. Quoted from Centers for Disease Control and Prevention. Web-based Injury Statistics Query and Reporting System (WISQARS) [Online]. (2013). National Center for Injury Prevention and Control, Centers for Disease Control and Prevention.

[3]   "Youth Suicide Statistics," The Parent Resource Program, The Jason Foundation, *JasonFoundation.com*, accessed August 15, 2016, http://jasonfoundation.com/prp/facts/youth-suicide-statistics/.

[4]   Tim Clinton, President of American Association of Christian Counselors, AACC Foundation newsletter web edition, September 20, 2016, http://www.aaccmail.net/w/VlH763F6L3C892HqcH8ojVtg1Q/8LelYuf0K8L4 0B2Q5JbJFA/fEV8923Ue5venYTYoMtETCkg.

Chapter 3

[5]   "Tattoo Statistics," Statistic Brain, accessed May 23, 2013, www.statisticbrain.com/tattoo-statistics.

[6]   Ruth E. Schneider and David S. Prudhomme, *From Stressed to Best: A Proven Program for Reducing Everyday Stress* ([Port Clinton, OH?]: Mederi Wellness Press, 2014), 19.

[7]   C. Beaulieu and C. Lebel, "Some Brain Wiring Continues to Develop Well Into Our 20s," Science Daily, September 23, 2011, accessed June 14, 2013, https://www.sciencedaily.com/releases/2011/09/110922134617.htm.

[8]   TJ Wray, *Surviving the Death of a Sibling: Living Through Grief When an Adult Brother or Sister Dies* (New York: Three Rivers Press, 2003), 1.

[9]   Ibid., 6.

Chapter 4

[10] Elisabeth Kübler Ross, *On Death and Dying* (New York: Macmillan, 1969).

[11] Ibid., 37.

[12] H. Norman Wright, Tangled Ball of Grief Laminated Cards, accessed June 20, 2013, https://www.hnormanwright.com/.

[13] "Guilt," *American Heritage Dictionary Online*, accessed November 19, 2016, https://ahdictionary.com/word/search.html?q=guilt.

[14] Simpson, J. A., and E. S. C. Weiner. "Regret." *The Oxford English Dictionary*. Second ed. 1989. Print.

[15] Colette Bouchez, "Serotonin: 9 Questions and Answers," Depression Health Center, *WebMD* Feature, Reviewed by Brunilda Nazario, MD, http://www.webmd.com/depression/features/serotonin.

[16] Randy Alcorn, *Heaven* (Wheaton, IL: Tyndale House, 2004), 312.

[17] "Understanding Depression—Prevention," reviewed by Joseph Goldberg, MD, on February 27, 2015, accessed July 15, 2015, http://www.webmd.com/depression/guide/understanding-depression-prevention.

[18] Daniel G. Amen, MD, *The Brain Warriors Way: Ignite Your Energy and Focus Attack Illness and Aging Transform Pain into Purpose (New York, NY:* New American Library, 2016), 102.

[19] Daniel G. Amen, MD, *Change Your Brain, Change Your Life: The Breakthrough Program for Conquering Anxiety, Depression, Obsessiveness, Lack of Focus, Anger, and Memory Problems* (New York: Three Rivers Press, 1998), 207.

[20] Jerry Sittser, *A Grace Disguised: How the Soul Grows through Loss* (Grand Rapids, MI: Zondervan, 1995), 33.

[21] Daniel G. Amen, MD, *Change Your Brain, Change Your Life: The Breakthrough Program for Conquering Anxiety, Depression, Obsessiveness, Lack of Focus, Anger, and Memory Problems* (New York: Three Rivers Press, 1998), 205.

[22] Daniel G. Amen, MD, *The Brain Warriors Way: Ignite Your Energy and Focus Attack Illness and Aging Transform Pain into Purpose* (New York: New American Library, 2016), 85

Chapter 5

[23] "Teens and Sleep," National Sleep Foundation, accessed August 15, 2015, https://sleepfoundation.org/sleep-topics/teens-and-sleep.

[24] "What Is Depression"? Depression and Bipolar Alliance, dbsahouston.org, accessed November 19, 2016, http://www.dbsahouston.org/what-is-depression?

[25] "Emotional and Psychological Trauma," *www.HelpGuide. org*, accessed August 30, 2015, http://www.helpguide.org/articles/ptsd-trauma/emotional-and-psychological-trauma.htm.

[26] Linda Brinser, "How Does Stress Affect the Immune System," Easy Stress Management, accessed August 20, 2015, http://www.stressaffect.com/how-does-stress-affect-the-immune-system.html.

27   John Eldridge, Ransomed Heart, Love God, Live Free monthly newsletter, August 2016

28   Alan Kirk and Steve King, *Trauma's Effect on the Brain, An Overview for Educators: Reclaiming School in the Aftermath of Trauma, Advise Based on Experience* (New York: Palgrave-Macmillan, 2012), 15.

29   HelpGuide.org, "Emotional and Psychological Trauma: Causes and Effects, Symptoms and Treatment," accessed August 30, 2015, http://www.healingresources.info/emotional_trauma_overview.htm.

30   Alan Kirk and Steve King, *Trauma's Effect on the Brain, An Overview for Educators: Reclaiming School in the Aftermath of Trauma, Advise Based on Experience* (New York: Palgrave-Macmillan, 2012), 15.

31   Lindsey Barton Straus, JD, "Concussion Recovery Starts with Both Physical and Cognitive Rest," MomsTeam.com, last modified December 15, 2015, accessed February 2, 2016, http://www.momsteam.com/concussion-physical-rest/concussion-recovery-starts-with-both-physical-and-cognitive-rest#ixzz4BxGrti00.

32   GriefShare, *Your Journey from Mourning to Joy* (Wake Forest, NC: Church Initiatives, 2014), 22.

Chapter 6

33   Molly Edmonds, "Are Teenage Brains Really Different from Adult Brains?" HowStuffWorks.com, last modified August 26, 2008, accessed September 15, 2015, http://science.howstuffworks.com/life/inside-the-mind/human-brain/teenage-brain1.htm.

34   GriefShare, *Your Journey from Mourning to Joy* (Wake Forest, NC: Church Initiatives, 2014) 122.

Chapter 7

35   Daniel AmenMD, *The Brain Warriors Way: Ignite Your Energy and Focus Attack Illness and Aging Transform Pain into Purpose* (New York: New American Library, 2016) 182

36 GriefShare, *Surviving the Holidays* (Wake Forest, NC: Church Initiatives, 2014).

37 https://www.lowes.com/projects/decorate-and-entertain/make-a-poinsettia-bloom-year-after-year/project

Chapter 10

38 Don Piper with Cecil Merphey, *90 Minutes in Heaven: A True Story of Death and Life* (Grand Rapids, MI: Revell, 2004).

39 Todd Burpo with Lynn Vincent, *Heaven is for Real: A Little Boy's Astounding Story of His Trip to Heaven and Back* (Nashville, TN: Thomas Nelson, 2010).

40 Randy Alcorn, *Heaven* (Wheaton, IL: Tyndale House, 2004)

41 Ibid., 16.

42 Ibid., 66.

43 Ibid., 67.

44 Ibid., 345.

45 Ibid., 69.

46 Ibid., 117.

47 Ibid., 388.

Starfish Story

48   adapted from *The Star Thrower*, by Loren Eiseley (1907 – 1977)

www.ingramcontent.com/pod-product-compliance
Lightning Source LLC
Chambersburg PA
CBHW030251030426
42336CB00009B/338